POETICA 2
The Noise Made by Poems

GW00640689

By Peter Levi

POETRY
Collected Poems 1955-1975   1976
Five Ages   1978
Private Ground   1981
The Echoing Green   1983

TRANSLATIONS
Yevtushenko: Selected Poems   1962
Pausanias: Guide to Greece   1971
The Psalms   1976
Pavlopoulos: The Cellar   1977
Marko the Prince (with Anne Pennington)   1983

FICTION
The Head in the Soup   1979

PROSE
The Light Garden of the Angel King   1973
The English Bible   1974
The Noise Made by Poems   1977
The Hill of Kronos   1980
Atlas of the Greek World   1980
The Flutes of Autumn   1983

Peter Levi

The Noise
Made by Poems

Anvil Press Poetry

First published in 1977
New edition published in 1984
by Anvil Press Poetry Ltd
69 King George Street London SE10 8PX
ISBN 0 85646 132 6 (hardback)
ISBN 0 85646 133 4 (paperback)

This book is published
with financial assistance from
The Arts Council of Great Britain

Printed and bound in England
at The Camelot Press Ltd, Southampton

FOR IANNIS TSIRKAS

Preface to Second Edition

I am surprised and delighted that this book, which has a didactic purpose and was based on cannibalized lectures, is now being reprinted. It was meditated with passion and written with great excitement. It was a waterfall of words, and in retrospect I can see why some readers thought it thin, fragmentary and puzzling. But it pleased those it was meant to please, and has slowly made its way in the world. It is in places helpful about simple but important problems. I would not like to expand it today, but to simplify it, if that were possible, and to comb out its paradoxes.

Of course there is a lot more to say. I would like to write a study of the sound of seriousness in German poets like Bobrowski, Huchel and Sabais, in whom it is the verbal expression of a deep sobriety. Poetry reveals truth as television reveals personality. It has a built in lie-detector. I would like to enter more deeply into the nature of lyric stanza form and the influence of music on words, first in the 1590s and then throughout the one long generation for which the same lyric impetus flourished, and stanza forms grew wild in every hedge, down to the Restoration. 'A nightingale the other night taught me a complex stanza form', as Oliver Bernard has put it. Poetry is a learned art. The same Mr Lawes wrote music for George Herbert, Andrew Marvell and John Milton. The language never saw such formal abundance and originality again until the poems of Thomas Hardy.

There are some arguments that need to be unknotted about Irish metre, and French metre, where the professional metrical scholars have set up too mechanical a system. But these arguments are extremely detailed and too technical for a book like this. Indeed I am convinced that they are often too technical to be true. The noise made by poems is heard in the ear, and relished and recognized at once, and it can be repeated by illiterate poets. The subtle chanting of the long lines of Balkan heroic poetry, and surely once upon a time the oceanic music of the *Iliad* and the *Odyssey*, are precisely the product of illiterate tradition; they lived only in the mouth and in the ear, yet one can hear them to this day. By contrast, even the greatest Renaissance theorists of poetry make little sense.

It seems to me more certain now than it did twenty or even five years ago that the crisis of the 1900s, when English poetry adopted an exaggerated, frantic stress rhythm (elsewhere the symbolists were crooning their verses), was a crisis of the language. The rot of excessive emphasis had started with Tennyson, who transmuted 'Sweet Master-gunner, split our keel in twain' into 'Sink me the ship, Master Gunner – sink her, split her in twain! Fall into the hands of God, not into the hands of Spain!' Kipling, Belloc, Henley, Masefield and many others used a similar heavily rhymed system that ignored quantity or length of syllable, and they perished by it; today the sound of their poems is tastelessly artificial and their great talents have shipwrecked. Bridges won through in tatters by his study of Milton, and Yeats was saved by his Irish accent. The tide turned when Ezra Pound reviewed a French book by Duhamel and Vildrac that suggested a quantitative element in modern poetry, and applied their ideas to his own writing.

We still call poetry writing, and the muddled work-sheets of poets show that we do so justly. And yet the training of Irish bards, which still existed in the eighteenth century, taught them to compose like blind men, alone in darkness. The sermons of John Donne lasted an hour; they were meticulously prepared for a week but written down only after preaching, never before. The style of Milton's poetry in his blindness is still magisterial in syntax as in everything else, but he seems to hang line on line and phrase on pendent phrase; it does sound like a blind poet's progression. Still, even when he could see, his work-sheets for 'Lycidas' were extremely clean and neat, as we hear that Shakespeare's were. When poetry is a habitual and a lifetime's exercise, it is like a language that has been learnt.

But Donne's sermons and the Irish bardic poems were essentially performances. One can hardly say the same of any of Milton's poems except *Comus* or maybe *Samson Agonistes*. And yet performed poems and particularly the stage have had a crucial influence on English, just as they did on Greek poetry. We still learn from Shakespeare and Marlowe; they define for us what poetry is. And in the poetry of Dryden, of Yeats and of Eliot, the theatre was a wooden muse, a technical inspiration, and an important part of their development, even if we judge that their theatrical verse was not in itself the most valuable. In our time the best poems are often private or spiritual; the poet as a private and expressive human being is the symbol of our salvation and our moral survival. Yet it is in the nature of poetry that it constantly seeks to be public. It is in the nature of the noise made by poems. We are refreshed by innocent music, but poetry awakens many other expectations.

PETER LEVI
June 1984

I

THE REMOTE ORIGINS of this book go back at least to 1966. By then I already had the idea of one day putting together some literary essays, chiefly because I regretted the ephemeral quality of various pieces I was publishing; but I would never have dared to confront the central issues of poetry, as I conceived them, in a complete book. What I am now presenting is not a thesis but a consideration of some important themes which are inter-related so that one has to be treated in terms of the others.

Of course all poets and most literary scholars think about poetry continually, both about the theory and about practical questions. The theoretic compartment of their thoughts is seldom more than the sparks struck off in a workshop; it is essentially a projection of something technical. This seems to be true of Dryden and Eliot and surely also of much lesser writers. The first time I was ever greatly impressed by any discussion of poetry apart from works of detailed scholarship was by Lorca's 'Theory and Function of the *Duende*', which I read as an undergraduate in about 1956 in a borrowed American translation. That is still at the bottom of what I believe about good poetry and bad, but there is no call for a weakened version of Lorca's splendid essay. Since then I have had many enthusiasms: for Rimbaud, Vallejo, Brecht, Nikos Gatsos, and a lengthening list of English and American poets. I have tried to quote only poets and lines I have genuinely come to feel a passion for. A book like this is not an anthology, but if the verses quoted seem like a bizarre and eclectic anthology, I can claim that they do at least represent personal experiences. The sort of verses I have quoted are the sort of verses I was thinking about when I considered these themes.

If I have made any special steps forward in understanding the art of· poetry, three at least of them have been connected with Greece. The first was when I visited that country in 1963. I had singled out from modern Greek poetry the line 'A little wheat for the festival, a little wine for memory, a little water for the dust'. It comes from a poem by Nikos Gatsos; I knew some Greek and for some reason the line meant a lot to me, and I managed to meet him. He told me, eating out of doors one windy August night, on the last night I was in Athens, about a surrealist game that he and Elytis used to play when they were young poets. There are three players, as in Consequences; each one in turn writes, turns down the top of the paper, and passes it on; the first writes a question, the second an answer, the third a comment. Read together, it is quite astonishing what coherence they can have. I had been thinking hard and unprofitably about how context is built up and brought to bear in a poem. This game successfully played furnishes a clue. It is easy to see how each sentence modifies the others, and how together they set up a powerful resonance their superficial meaning could never account for. Playing this game during an English political crisis we once produced: 'What is Teddy Heath doing now?' 'She has retired to a tapestry monastery.' 'The goldfish in the fishpond are too fat and pink to bother about.' That first night in Athens produced phrases like 'sleeping sometimes in the foliage of the vineyard', and 'I am a secret mountain'. I have been told that the same game still flourishes in Romania.

The other two steps I took in Greece were the experience of Crete, where a more or less epic tradition is still alive, and secondly quite a long friendship and a longer study and admiration of George Seferis. It was he who first raised in a way I could understand the moral element in aesthetic matters. It was in the study of his poetry that I found it useful to try to isolate and discuss his tone of voice. He is a forceful example of what the development of a poet can be, how enormously his range and depth can increase. He was a poet in some ways as dry as Larkin, but his stature was mountainous. He was one of the greatest writers in this century in any language, and if that is a claim impossible to substantiate to readers not lucky enough to know modern Greek, then so much the worse for them. From Seferis it was possible to learn or believe one was learning what seriousness about poetry is. His mastery of the problems of language, particularly in Greek but communicably even in English, was unique, and it was an extraordinary phenomenon. He taught you how to hear your language in the way that an eighteenth-century sailor could pick out intuitively the sound of every strain or creak or squeak in a great ship at sea.

Most of what there is to learn about poetry has to be learnt in one's own language. But it is mostly learnt by reading and turning over poems in one's head, and little by deliberate criticism. Or to put it another way, criticism works more by selection and reselection, and by nosing hungrily about for new materials and new things to say, than it does by long analytic treatments. Seen with hindsight, it seems less important in what order one discovered poems and read books than that one did so discover and so read. It is in adolescence and youth that every new passion seems so overwhelming, and the whole of life seems to change overnight at least once in every summer. Later we all wander backwards and forwards over the same few centuries and languages slowly deepening and widening what we know, and using at any one time whatever nature and circumstance give us an appetite and a need to use. No doubt celibacy puts a keener edge on the appetite and a wider scope on the wandering, but that of course is no argument for celibacy.

Under the few centuries of English poetry we know there lies an important history and social history. For the understanding of how social history affects language and poetry, and how a political issue might underlie a crisis of form in writing, I owe as much as the rest of the world to Lukács, whose writings I have known only since the sixties when they began to appear in English. I have also taken a number of hints from John Berger. But I have done my best to suppress in this book any clear analysis of English and European social history, or of what our crisis is about. That is firstly because I am not sure I am right about it, and the long drawn out self-contradictions of my position would be boring and anyway belong to a quite different book. But secondly, I think that as much as I say in this book is or ought to be common ground. If there are remoter conclusions to be drawn, let the reader draw them for himself. I wanted to speak about poetry and how poetry reflects reality, not so much about the reality it reflects.

I have written twice elsewhere about the history of poetry in English and of the language: wildly about poetry in an introduction to Pope, and more soberly about the language in an introduction to the old versions of the Bible in English. But the history of what has happened in English, the graph of change and the crisis-marks, are not directly relevant to this book, though they might confirm its conclusions. I have therefore not repeated or adapted that material although I have not scrupled to pillage some occasional writings. I would have liked to incorporate a lecture given in 1969 at Princeton and again in 1970 in

Athens, called 'Mr Seferis' Tone of Voice'. It treats the marrow of my subject, and it might have been as well to include one study of a particular poet in fuller detail. But the problem of quotation in modern Greek was insuperable. I have tried to quote poems in their original languages; some who will not know one language will know another, but very few readers of this book are likely to know modern Greek. My own experience both of poetry and of life has been so much bound up with Greece, particularly in the last ten years, that I have inevitably referred often to Greek literature; rightly or wrongly I thought that a full-scale treatment of George Seferis would overbalance it altogether. On the other hand there was no other single poet I wanted to write about as much.

I had thought of discussing Quasimodo, who wrote one of my favourite lines: 'e le parole nate fra le vigne' ['and the words born from the vineyards']. But there is something so subtle about his virtues, something so liquid about his tone, that his poems resist any critical incision. It is not always the greatest poets one likes best, and even those one likes best are not always easy to write about. If I had spoken more about the influence of content on poetry, or given freer play to my personal preferences, I would have written something about Francis Jammes and René Guy Cadou. If I had dealt more with political poetry I would have written some admiring paragraphs about Yevtushenko. I would also have liked to write something about contemporary leftist English poetry and its unexpected virtues and vices. Adrian Mitchell has driven his poetry to an extreme position where it only just continues to be poetry at all, but on the margins of the music-hall he has made the most brilliant formal inventions of any poet of his generation. Christopher Logue has brought together his startling talents only in a free adaptation of some books of the *Iliad*, a work as powerful as the rest of left-wing poetry, with very few exceptions, is impotent.

Much more could have been said about the conditions of heroic poetry, but the subject is in the melting-pot, and it would be a different book. The techniques of oral poetry are not in fact difficult to reproduce by imitation, but they are much more difficult to write about. It used to take three years from the moment of vocation, usually in a dream, and acceptance as an apprentice, to become a heroic poet in Soviet central Asia, but after three years in a western university one would hardly have finished the most tenuous thesis. There is a similar difference between the understanding of ballad poetry as a performing art, even as a combined poet and musician, and the analytic, articulate study of the same ballads for a learned periodical. Writing like Homer is not only morally and by a natural hierarchy better than writing about him; were it not that Homeric Greek is a dead language it would even be easier.

If there is any one basis of this book which has been to me a discovery, it is that the simplest verse and the simplest elements in verse respond better to probing than does what we call 'great' poetry. For years I used to walk about with a few lines of some great poet in my head, throwing them against the walls of my skull and trying to find out what they were made of. I tried the trick of replacing words and seeing what difference it made, but as I then understood nothing about how the power of context works in poetry, this taught me little, and as my verbal memory is bad, I ended up very confused. Incidentally the power of context in passages of intensely written prose, the battlefield of Waterloo in *Vanity Fair* for example, or Evelyn Waugh's description of the fall of Crete in *Officers and Gentlemen*, or most of *Middlemarch*, accumulates in the same mysterious, that is invisible and irrational, and suddenly ineluctable way. But to observe this, whether in prose or in verse, the simplest examples are best. What seems extraordinary and most interesting is that so many characteristics of the whole spectrum of poetry from the greatest to the least are determined by such tiny and obvious factors as a repeated noise. And yet it must be so, or we should not be using the one word poetry for such a wide range of performances in so many languages. What poems have in common cannot but be fundamental to poetry.

It is worth giving two more words of warning. I was once present at a discussion between a poet of outstanding honesty and authority and a university teacher of celebrated intelligence. They were talking about greatness in poetry, and the university teacher was eagerly probing into the poet's views, offering one well calculated example after another, and plainly enjoying the intellectual canter. The poet was rising to every dry fly, and he looked in considerable disarray, like a fish about to be reeled in. The conversation ended somehow, and as we left the poet said of his friend, 'You know I like that man, but he raises subjects that are too big for him.' The point I want to make is not that academic men are likelier to do so than poets; in fact the opposite is the case, and pretentiousness is far more a besetting sin of poets than it is of academics. The point is simply that greatness if glibly treated crumbles to nothing, and if it is seriously treated is a subject above most of us for most of our lives. It is better to speak about what is genuine. That may be a lower category, though I think it is as honourable, but it is certainly sufficiently difficult to occupy our time.

Of those who go to museums, some of the public prefer always what is grandiose and different from their own lives. A hatchet-faced lady surveying his Grace's curtains is a nasty sight. There are some who prefer what is subtly close to their own lives, but also more subtly distant: school-teachers watching eighteenth-century farm carts as if they were animal, and fathers of families with their children wandering past huge old industrial machinery. There are also those who are simply hungry for whatever feeds them, wherever they can find it. Of this last class the most sophisticated are the most false. All this is an allegory of poetry. My book is meant for the second class of people; it is written in the belief that to understand a farm cart or an old mill-wheel is the best beginning, and that however complicated a tradition of art may become, what is done in it is done intuitively from old models and the elements are simple. Understanding poetry is more like understanding an eighteenth-century farm cart than it is like understanding a picture by Rubens.

It will be seen that I share the common puritanic prejudice that the less said about poetry the better. If there were something really complicated that could be known about poetry I would distrust its usefulness. This is not to decry great scale and formality. I read Milton more than most poets, though I have never read the whole of Spenser and there are some kinds of formality I am unable to cope with however much I love the poet. In the same way I have friends I love to spend an evening with, but I would not wear court dress in order to do so. And between thick and thin textures of poetry, between rich elaborate poems and poor but honest ones, I find myself in the position of the man who would rather cut off his hand than choose between the sheep and the goats, but if he had to choose he would choose the goats. The character of poetry itself, let alone of poets, is more goat-like than sheep-like, and even the mildest of institutional poets are goats in sheep's clothing.

There was a young Jesuit poet in the early eighteenth century who wrote a poem that swept Europe and was translated into many languages. It was about a convent parrot that repeated edifying phrases and was sent to a sister-house to show off. Unfortunately it travelled by canal, and picked up some popular language that caused trouble in the convent parlour. In spite of the fact that in the poem the parrot repents and dies a holy death, the young man was expelled from the Jesuits. Voltaire, who liked the poem, was delighted and said 'One poet more and one Jesuit less'. The saint of poetry in this story is not so much the young man as the parrot. There is a certain frivolity about what are in fact important themes in the conception of the poem. It was the parrot that lived and died, even without the benefit of human intelligence, in a desperate attempt to express reality as language. I know of a Prussian archaeologist in the American army during the Second World War, who left behind him on a Pacific island a translation of the *Iliad* into the local language. That was a heroic enterprise; it might even be productive. There is nothing so wanted and so unavailable in the world as poets of authority to show with passion what the world is really like.

2

ANY POET who takes his trade seriously is likely to be continually rewriting in his head the whole history of poetry. What an inspection of those thoughts at any one time would reveal might well be like the short notes a novelist will write. His view of other writers would be dramatic, it would alter, it would be workshop shavings. It would include a thorough study or a magnified consciousness of certain details. In fact it would be something like a continually altering film-script. The questions and the values the writer was dramatizing in his reading or memory of other writers, and in the whole endless process of sorting out reality, would arise directly from problems in his own work, which is also of course a process of making sense of reality. You cannot express reality without implicitly making sense of it. This operation is essentially concrete but it throws off a moral atmosphere in which enormous questions are half-seen to be standing around it, as they are in the written film treatment, which is not exactly a shooting script, for Eisenstein's ruined masterpiece, *Que Viva Mexico!*

The way in which questions about other writers arise while a novelist is at work, how vast the issues are, and how the position or value of individual works can appear to shift, appears very well in a note by Scott FitzGerald for *The Last Tycoon*, the novel he was at work on when he died. Had he finished his novel this note might well have been thrown away; it is interesting because in it one can see the writer at work, and his consciousness of literature altering as he works.

'Object: I wanted a seduction—very Californian, yet new—very Hollywood, say. If he has no illusion, he has at least great pity and excitement, friendliness, stimulus, fascination.

Where will the warmth come from in this? Why does he think she's warm? Warmer than the voice in *Farewell to Arms*. My girls were all so warm and full of promise. What can I do to make it honest and different?

The sea at night. Como. St-Pol (used in *Tender*). Why are French romances cold and sad *au fond*?—why was Wells warm?'

Something analogous to this note is often present in the heads of poets. It appears in a rationalized form in their critical essays: for example in Yeats' introduction to the old *Oxford Book of Modern Verse*, and in Thom Gunn's selection of Ben Jonson. Even inside poems Robert Lowell in his *Notebook* and in his *History* is much preoccupied with a shifting dialogue of the same kind. But every modern poet is also inevitably a modern man, and his preoccupations and duties and questions are human before they are those of a poet. He may well fail to make sense of modern reality but he would be chicken-witted not to try, and not to use every available instrument. Brecht tried to make sense in poetry of the Communist Manifesto. Poets are not unaware of criticism, of science, of philosophy, even of economics, though some of the plunges they take into these subjects are as ill-advised as those of more prudent people. Maybe poets are particularly vulnerable to systematic errors, because too often their attention to such matters is secondary: they are trying to make poems, and if some complicated instrument helps the poems to work, they will have a fatal subconscious attraction to that instrument. To do them justice, Pound's attention to economics, Yeats' to spiritualism, Eliot's to Anglo-Catholicism, Brecht's to Marxism, do not betray any lack of attention, but specialists in those four subjects might say it was attention of a particular kind.

The work of poets is determined by an inward hunger, and we value them passionately when our hunger corresponds to theirs. In the course of an average lifetime more than one poet can teach you a new hunger you had never known you had, or you had forgotten. It is virtuous to be hungry. In this way poets in their succession, and in our successive reading of them, define our natures. Unhappy the nation that has no poets good enough to do that. If we were confined to modern poetry in America and England, that would be an insufficient diet, but we can range backward in time and through other languages. The fact that in the course of the ordinary twists of human growth we furiously reject today what we loved yesterday is less important. The fact that in the complaisance of middle age we return to old toys has no importance at all. By that time of life we are trying among other things to understand a self and a development we can no longer accurately remember. Anything that expresses reality will be useful sooner or later and more than once. Falsity withers away, or it ought to, simply because of its lack of usefulness. Fustian wears thin, fulfilled rhetoric does not.

The passionate moral acceptance or rejection we feel from time to time about some poet, for example, about such a poet as Allen Ginsberg or about Kipling, has to do with a developing sense of reality. It would be interesting to get this judgement right, and that demands a high degree of attention to the individual poet, and perhaps some knowledge of history as well. Critics of poetry usually imply common assumptions about the whole framework of history and morality, and sometimes philosophy as well. But the poet at his stove among clouds of moral steam does not necessarily share these assumptions. Further, he is likely to be oddly informed: there is no generally accepted corpus of knowledge in these days, and he is likely to be more selective than most. A poet today if he cared at all for trees and birds would have broken the husk of Tennysonian nature; his knowledge might well be less convincing than Tennyson's fine and delicate observation of a shared environment, but it would certainly, if he cared to make it so, be more specific. The same might be true about his moral reading of history and of the modern world. To imagine is to some extent to accept, that is to conceive a thing to be real. It is hard to penetrate the work of a strange poet imaginatively without accepting his moral sensibility, and that comes close to the poet's profound and ramified relationship with the reality he expresses. A little unacceptable hysteria, a little poverty of judgement in the poet, and one might be tempted to reject that entire structure. The reader's conscience will supply him with his own examples.

On the other hand it is obvious enough that we read poetry with an open mind, and most of us read it most at the age when our minds are most open. Every poet has at some time said to his poem 'Speak against bonds . . . Go out and defy opinion', as Ezra Pound puts it in 'Commission'. But it is also true as he says in 'Au Salon',

> I suppose there are a few dozen verities
> That no shift of mood can shake from us.

There are things said that one can accept and begin to imagine and so to discover in oneself or in the world, only by first encountering them in a poem. The immense popularity of Gerard Manley Hopkins as a poet, the kind of greatness we sense in him as a poet, makes available to us something lost from our own lives, something we could not otherwise have. What Pound says goes for all poets: 'I mate with my free kind upon the crags.' Poetry does create a certain freedom, but this freedom is interior, moral, and hard to describe. It includes a sense of freshness and energy that are almost physical. It is the reward of confronting nature, recognizing reality, something very often more sensed than articulated even in the lines of a poem. There is an intensity about it which is not the normal condition of consciousness. There is also a stillness.

> I mate with my free kind upon the crags;
>   the hidden recesses
> Have heard the echo of my heels,
>   in the cool light,
>   in the darkness.

('Tenzone')

I believe that this quality of freedom is at the root of that curious old controversy about the relation between poetry and prayer. There are certainly prayers which are poems; for example the last canto of the *Divine Comedy* and some of Villon's poems are both, and so are a few poems by Herbert, by Donne, and by Vaughan. They have the form of prayers, poetry being voracious, even omnivorous, of traditional forms of speech. But they work as other poems do, they are more like other poems than other prayers. They are exactly calculated rhythmic structures of precise words, and they express reality, not necessarily religious doctrine, but something we know to be genuine independently of sectarian belief. But what prayer does is to present God to the soul or the soul to God; if it expresses reality it simply happens to do so, and if it achieves liberty, as in some sense perhaps only prayer can do, then it does so scarcely articulately, and quite silently. One is not a higher form of the other or a substitute for the other, they are different. Poetry is language, and the moral liberty it effects is just as like what is attained by understanding as it is like what is attained in prayer. If the most moving prayers are poems, which I do not personally believe, that is because more or less anything that is said can be better said in a poem. The context that a poem sets up is also a moral context.

The wonderful poetry of John of the Cross has popular roots and the best of it has little obvious dogmatic content. The language of *The Song of Songs* had already in its use in the Bible a strange and attractive ambiguity. Throughout the middle ages it was a source of secular love poetry as well as religious rhapsody. The interpenetration of pastoral poetry, an erotic sense, and the most mysterious of religious aspirations was already established in popular and learned tradition. What John of the Cross contributed was a freshness and a crispness hard to distinguish from his life and his moment in time. Typically of such questions as this, it is important that he was early to seize on the possibilities of formal Renaissance metres in Spanish, and perhaps equally important that he was much affected by the traditional popular songs that he heard sung in the street. The metrical form of poems, something living which it is impossible to exhaust in description, is more important to how poetry works than any religious aspiration can be. That may be no more than a kind of breathing of the soul that troubles the surface, but the subject-matter of poetry is defined by the words the poet uses, it is as concrete as something painted.

Poetry has a special relation to music. A sentence said and a sentence sung differ both obviously and subtly. The song by Campion 'My sweetest Lesbia let us live and love' is already a fine poem on the printed page, but music transforms it. The pitch of words in English is important in conversation, and more so in poetry; so is the comparative length and shortness of syllables, and so of course is the stress accent on words. Taken together with certain silences and certain fulfilled expectations of the ear, with the subconscious expectations of the language itself and with what is particularly expected in given forms of speech, in a love poem for example, all this is a great part of the technical repertory of poetry. But music affects a poem by holding natural pitch in suspension, by altering stress and length and imposing a new kind of rhythm. Neither rhyme nor assonance remain unaffected, they sound differently. New expectations imposed by the music overlie what a metrical stress pattern and the language and meaning had already imposed. It is not surprising that the discovery of the Italian art of madrigal had an enormous influence in Elizabethan England on newly felt metrical values of which poets as well as song-writers had become conscious.

Perhaps a song must inevitably be first a poem, but music is a metamorphosis. And yet some shadow of music seems to fall on many traditional ideas about poems. I once asked a distinguished old man in his eighties why we read poetry and he replied 'Because it sings to one what one wants to hear of'. What gives ballad poetry its powerful fascination, if not the formality and strength of old and traditional language that fitted itself by a natural, almost organic tendency to a simple and traditional music? It is important to notice that when this simplicity comes to be analysed it turns out to be far more complex and subtle than what an individual of original genius could invent on his own, but that is always the nature of traditional form. It is as true of craftsmanship, of a flint hand-axe or the handle of a scythe, as it is of verbal forms, of rituals and of music. In all these cases there is a whole social context which is brought to bear on the form. When the social context is dead, some smell of it or some ghost of it can linger for a long time in popular tradition. The strength of what survives will derive from a society which patient scholarship may laboriously reconstruct, but the strength itself is immediately present to us, and in the case of ballads at times even without music. In the case of work-songs the music is implicit, one can all but hear it, or maybe what one can sense is some musical sublimation of the rhythm of the work:

> Well he chopped with a hatchet, Great Godamighty,
> Well he choppin' with a axer, Oh my Lord.

If those two lines were merely literary, one would still have to say that the syncopation of their rhythm and pitch-accent was essentially musical and highly inventive. They come in fact, as the reader may have guessed, from a collection of Afro-American work-songs from Texas prisons. It is easy enough, or at least possible, to supply the context in popular musical tradition and in society that these verses live by, but their strength presents itself immediately. Indeed, as often happens with genuine popular work-songs, their inevitable qualities are so strong as to drive any other qualities away.

In ballad poetry there is a kind of music that feeds the sense of the lines even when it is not heard, just as surely as Campion's music feeds the words of his songs even if one has never heard the music.

> An earthly nourris sits an sings,
> And aye she sings, Ba, lily wean!
> Little ken I my bairnis father,
> Far less the land that he staps in.

There is something unearthly about this first verse, perhaps suggested by the word 'earthly', and something desolate, so that one is almost unsurprised when the 'father' turns up in the next verse. The whole structure and impetus of the verse seems to me to be essentially musical.

> I am a man, upo the lan,
>   An I am a silkie in the sea;
> And when I'm far and far frae lan,
>   My dwelling is in Sule Skerrie.

In the Lesbia song by Campion that I have already mentioned there is the same slight musical syncopation of the formal metre, the same seductive slight dragging of some of the syllables. It was surely the musical quality of Campion's consciousness of particular syllabic values that made possible his masterly refrain and the closing two lines, in which he transmutes his whole poem, acceptably betraying the great original by Catullus on which he bases it. His sense of a song very properly overmasters his obligation to Latin poetry, and it does so for musical, not for sentimental reasons.

> And Lesbia close up thou my little light,
> And crowne with love my ever-during night.

How different is Louise Labé's sonnet treatment of the same poem by Catullus: 'Baise-m'encor, rebaise moy et baise . . .'

To go back for a moment to Scott FitzGerald, there is clear enough evidence that in writing this song and this poem, Campion was as actively considering and criticizing Catullus and Propertius, and as intensely meditating on the kind of song he wanted to write. Incidentally, Campion was happy with this poem, which stands first in his *A Booke of Ayres* (1601), but there is another, much less good version in Corkine's *Second Booke of Ayres* (1612), which may be an early sketch of Campion's song. His editor Vivian believed it was by Campion, but there is much less of subtle musicality about it. Whatever is the truth about this, the point stands that many kinds of intense preoccupation arise like steam off a horse from the development of a poet, and that many judgements are implicit in the concrete result, the poetry, and they are implicitly or sometimes articulately communicated to the reader. Many truths and perhaps some falsities have been crumbled together to create the style of Virgil in the *Aeneid*; they can still be sensed, and to analyse them out is one of the purposes of Virgilian scholarship. The style of John Berryman is as complex and it has an urgent contemporary importance; in neither case is it possible to make a prose translation which is remotely equivalent to the poem. In fact Berryman's poems are often their own best prose translation.

That implies that what a poem is must usually be different from even the whole of what it means or articulately says, just as what a song is or does, how it works, must be different from the written words of which it might consist. Analysis is always secondary to the poem itself, but what is the poem? It is not what was in the poet's head, or his intentions, or his vision, it is not even his words. He can and often will alter all these, they are an irrecoverable process of which the final result is the poem as he publishes it or leaves it in writing. A poem is the text of a poem. No one reading of it has authority over another except so far as the text implies one interpretation. Apollinaire believed that a good poem would impose one special way of reading it even if you left out the punctuation. He might in principle be right, and it is certainly true that if every technical element of poetry, that is every factor in human language, were held in control in a poem, there would only be one way of reading it; other ways could be shown to be wrong. As it is there are lyric poems which permit of less variety of interpretation than speeches in Shakespeare, and there are modern poems we know so well that a reading by the poet himself can add little beyond the grain of his voice. And yet that little is an important little. The alphabet, the arrangement of lines, and the uses of punctuation, even with a fine and accustomed ear for rhythms do not always constitute an unambiguous notation for how poems ought to sound. There are cases in older poetry where we may be badly at sea. But the fact that this poetry works at all, and works immediately, is a demonstration that we do sense it and that we can judge it. The demonstration is empirical.

Experience means a lot. Poetry is essentially something you are used to: you become used to it very early in life, and since then you have extended your range with new examples so that all the poems you have ever come across taken together form a massive vocabulary of what poetry is and what it can do. To write poems is to add to the corpus of works you have defined together as poetry. But one may still stumble into some new area of poems, recognizable but in some way strange, where the examples are too few and the rules seem to have altered and the whole aesthetic system seems hard to grasp. It may be a matter of ear, say in Anglo-Saxon poetry or in the earliest Latin, or it may be a matter of conventions, as it might be in the linked *haiku* of Basho. It might also be a moral and a historical matter, as it is for example to understand the impetus and the moral direction of the *Iliad* or of the Greek medieval poet Romanos. It is hard to know how we learn a new kind of poetry. Perhaps the point of entry into it is unimportant, but it seems that in every kind of poetry there is a coherence of one value in tension with another, a coherence of sounds and a system of language that might almost be articulated as rules. But scholarship can discover rules only a scholar can understand; poetry is intuitive rather than scholarly, and most poets are somewhat anarchic in their art. There are no instruments for understanding poetry except a hunger of the intelligence and of the ear.

There is no limit to how much knowledge and experience of life one ought to bring to reading a poem. A poem is never self-contained, it exists in the language and in the world. There is no objection at all to using what you know of a poet's personal life, except that it may well be misleading. But we read poets as well as poems: the alternative would be an interminable anthology of anonymous works. That would make nonsense of poetry because in most human language and almost all surviving poems except for epic and ballad poetry a particular speaker is implied: a particular human voice. The study of a poet includes a study of the coherence and inter-relations and development of his poetry. There is something not only disappointing but appalling and almost physical about lack of development in a poet. This is perhaps because in our world no work is permanent, there is an ennui about neo-classical perfection, we are unable to live with it. All that an artist can do is produce a life-work, an archive of imperfect works, a series of notes about how, in a world which makes no sense, reality can still be expressed. I believe this to be even truer of a poet like Eliot than of an expressionist poet. Development is human, it is a just moral expectation. One ought not to stress any social or political explanation, because there has always been a development in personal poets. Anonymous genius is not rare in ancient works of art or even in English poetry, and in ballads conceived of as anonymous, as in epic poetry, the moment of the tradition is nearly everything, individual sensibility is less important. But even within living tradition and at a time when poetry was not far from existing only in performances which constantly varied, there was a development. The *Odyssey* is very different from the *Iliad*. Society and the gods of society were altering fast at that time.

That is development as vast as a movement of the ocean and maybe as uncontrollable, but the development of an individual writer, say of Horace or of Basho, or to take a more uneven career the development of Mayakovsky, can be understood in terms of our knowledge of human beings outside the art of poetry. The poet may reach an impasse, but if his development has been honest we may feel as deeply for his silence as we did for his voice. Most people have thought there was an attractive peacefulness about the last years of Shakespeare, and I hope it may have been so. There are several ways of interpreting the final silence of Rimbaud, but they all reflect backwards on his poetry. Death on the other hand changes nothing; it is a blank edge, it limits the number of books on a shelf. There is a special dryness and force, and a special urgency and quietness, about the last poems of the great and old, which not all poets achieve: indeed there is a recognizable human greatness about this which inclines us more easily to name an artist as great. Maybe as we are hungry for hidden benefits in poetry so we are hungry for this early winter maturity in the lives of poets. John Berryman spoke of it in his elegy for William Carlos Williams.

> Too many journeys lie for him ahead,
> too many galleys & page-proofs to be read,
> he would like to lie down
> in your sweet silence, to whom was not denied
> the mysterious late excellence which is the crown
> of our trials & our last bride.
>
> ('The Dream Songs', 324)

We should read whole poets, and always whole poems, yet it is sometimes possible to dislodge the universe with one line. A poem is a process in time, it takes a measured time to read it or say it, longer to study it. Even if it commands an intense attention, though attention has no absolute, reading the poem is a piece of your life, like other pieces. But something on which a minimal unit of human attention can focus, which can be held complete in the mind with all its parts present, say one or two lines or a phrase, can sometimes serve as a criterion for how good a poem or a poet is. One can say of it, this could only be by So-and-so, or one can become hypnotized by a trick of rhythm or the thud of a truth. It used to be fashionable at the beginning of the century to judge poetry too much by the density of these wonderful snatches, to the detriment of the understanding of poems. But there really is something breathtaking about some of those well-known and often quoted fragments. I have never got over such a phrase as 'And after many a summer dies the swan', although Tennyson is not my favourite poet and this isolated quotation does the poem it comes from ('Tithonus') no justice. In its proper place its rhythm is slightly more robust and the swan is less mysterious.

Poetry is a discourse, it is committed to being continuous. Such a very long poem as Wordsworth's *Prelude* can do what no lesser extension would have done; without the faults of its length we would have lost one of those formative and satisfying works of art which nothing else can replace. In my case it was a winter's reading thirteen years ago that I still remember. Poems that have to be read over a long period need qualities different in kind from those of dramatic poetry or metaphysical lyrics. But however short a poem is it must need to use its whole length, it must bite its form to the bone. It was the flaccidity of a form too easily filled that led to the death-bed of the English sonnet; the sonnet is dying or has died of fatty degeneration of the heart. There are counter-examples, notably by Robert Lowell, but Lowell's form is closer to Rimbaud than to Wordsworth or Milton; it is really a new form altogether. His collection *History* is a splendid example of poems of continuous discourse: it is not only that every line, but that every poem, as a poem in its progression, is a continuous movement of intelligent muscles. They provoke to passionate acceptance or rejection, to argument or sometimes to silence as conversation would, but more effectively. In this they do their technical work as poems, and they express reality in a way that Ted Hughes in *Crow* seems to me to have failed to do. But that implies my judgement about reality; I have no confidence that I am right. It is difficult to assess poems justly. What is important is that they should at least have realities to talk about: that is what we expect of any discourse that attracts attention to itself.

The next question to ask is in what way poetry expresses the world. In the language of Shakespeare you have the sense of a poet expressing everything in the world. This is obviously possible only because Shakespeare is a dramatic poet, but the universality and the inclusiveness of his poetry are not strictly a function of dramatic situations, though the two are closely connected, and in fact the subject-matter, and Shakespeare's inbuilt attitude to things, thought, stories, individuals, and social forces do determine his range and genius as a poet. But what Shakespeare expresses is in language. It is a dry paradox to say that poems consist of words, but poetry does consist of language, and poetry can behave in more or less any way in which language can behave. Different kinds of poetry are equivalent simply to different habits or functions of language. Poetry is language heightened by insistent sounds or repeated rhythms: the degree of seriousness, accuracy, and economy which poetry demands is something demanded of the poet not as a poet but as a human being: these demands are a law of language, just as the laws of reason are laws of language. It is a question of the way we conspire to expect and demand, in the long tradition of our native speech, that the language shall be used. Once you use language consciously and intently you cannot escape the special demands that are inbuilt into poetry. The more intense the language is, the more strongly the demand is felt. The seriousness is moral and sentimental.

But language is inherited, and so these demands and these laws have always pre-existed in the language of some older generation: in the roots of the particular language we speak. This is what makes Shakespeare a national poet: his enormous vocabulary and his very strong sense of the sound and behaviour of English make him a kind of embodiment of the language itself, at least of a wider range of English than any other English writer. There is a sense in which the same might be said of the early versions of the English Bible. It would be true to say that Shakespeare expresses the world by means of including a number of different levels of language, and by ranging over a wide area of linguistic behaviour. The question is, what is the combination, what makes the English language in Shakespeare become poetry, how does Shakespeare's poetry express the world? Shakespeare's greatness as a poet, which I suppose is something that releases his fundamental quality and goodness, like that of wood, is in a way inseparable from the native genius of the English people, because it is inseparable from the bone and substance of English, and a language, in its vocabulary, its proverbs and in all its behaviour is the creation of the people. Poetry can express the world only because and in so far as language is a net that covers the world. There are certain tones of voice in language and in poetry—the Petrarchan love-sonnet for example—in which only certain kinds of reality can be conveyed; there are special languages or sub-languages which are limited in the same way: the literary epic language of Milton, for example, in which you have to call a telescope Galileo's glazed optic tube, or the language of the admirably skilful nineties poets and the Georgian poets, which being essentially an upper class idiom was inadequate to express the realities either of peace or of war. The poetry of Shakespeare expresses more of the world than any other English poetry because of the co-existence of many kinds and levels of language in his work imitating in their relationship tensions which are present in the actual world. I am not saying that his language is a mirror of social forces, which no doubt by hindsight we can see that it is, but that his understanding of reality, his secret art as a poet, was actually identical with his sense of what the English language is.

Expression of the world is not confined to dramatic poetry. The whole development of English poetry, if it is analysed in a similar way, gives the same results. I am not speaking only of simple lyrics, but time and time again all poetry moves towards a singleness of tone, a unity of language, which a social critic might relate to the rise of the middle classes, and a literary critic might admire for the subtlety and flexibility and civilization of which unity of language is a prerequisite. This tendency already exists in Gower's *Confessio Amantis* and in the court poetry of Chaucer, and more so in his disciples; Surrey's poetry is rather single-toned, Wyatt's not. Jacobean tragedy in its decadence was reducing itself towards a single tone, a self-distillation which was not far from self-parody. Pope seems to me an opposite example: a poet whose greatness depends on the very wide scope and reach and diversity of his language; the surface is smooth only in the same way as the hexameter poems of Horace: neither Pope nor Horace is a Parnassian writer. Pope has his limits, but he does express a huge slice of the real world; so does Byron in *Don Juan*. Clough expresses reality to a degree, but his language is purely that of the upper-middle class: he uses that language flexibly, and his device of an exchange of letters brings him near to dramatic poetry, but in fact it is the unity of his language which destroys him as a poet. Too much has been sacrificed in England to smoothness, both in poetry and in life.

The modern master of variety of texture in poetry, or at least the first such master in English is Thomas Hardy. The texture of his language is like the bark of an elm tree. Hardy can write like a gnarled provincial Victorian, but the genuineness and the honest confrontation of ironies and truths which are so impressive in him communicate themselves at the level of language. It is surely significant that Hardy, in whose poetry many levels and kinds of language co-existed, and whose art had roots in the life and songs of the labouring poor, should have achieved as a personal style, in the cracked looking-glass of his poems, an expression of the world just as he described it in terms of subject-matter and social reality in his prose. There is no place here to make any profound enquiry into Thomas Hardy's language, but I am not alone in believing that such an enquiry would be worth making. Thomas Hardy's star is at last in the ascendant. We are bound to return continually to the problems of contemporary or near-contemporary writers.

The great question is best looked at historically because what we are speaking of, the co-existence of a rich variety of fields of language in one poem, is not simply a matter of modern style, although it might easily seem to be if one started from its greatest modern virtuoso, James Joyce in *Ulysses*. It hardly matters whether you call that book a novel or a poem—I suppose you would have to call *Finnegans Wake* a poem, and *Ulysses* might perhaps be called a prose epic—but at any rate its influence on poets has not been negligible. William Carlos Williams' *Paterson* has something in common with *Ulysses*, although the particular combination of levels of language in *Paterson* may appear, at least to one less sensitive to American speech, to be looser and more a matter of hazard than in *Ulysses*. After Williams came Allen Ginsberg; the interest of his poetry depends very largely on its language-range, but the range is narrower than that of Joyce; there is sometimes a monotonous informality, reflecting the unity of language of a social sub-group: it is a special language which can express the world only in its own analysis. But the poetry does work and at once; the communication of what is genuine is irrefutable; analysis comes later.

One might consider in more detail the commingling of languages in the work of David Jones; we know or we may easily imagine that the origins of his style depend more or less directly on a reading of Joyce, some years after the First World War. He seems to have found through Joyce or in common with Joyce for the first time a medium that could express his own experiences as a private soldier. It was then that he wrote *In Parenthesis*, possibly the only poem in English since the middle ages that we have the right to call epic and Homeric. What he took from Joyce was a concentrated stylistic solution: a certain rhythm which he then developed for himself in one direction while Joyce in *Finnegans Wake* developed in another, a sense of tones of language and how one opens out into another, and an idea of how by a series of contrasts to convey an epic magnitude in modern writing. The fragmented texture of David Jones' poetry in *The Anathemata* and in parts of *In Parenthesis*, the oblique relationships of sentences, the strangeness and non-ordinariness of his writing, are inevitable consequences of his first discoveries. What he has in common with *Ulysses* is a compressed dramatic poetry (not the only or perhaps the chief characteristic of that book), and through it a way of relating the present to the past, the living to the dead, and the details of everyday life to a vast perspective. Here is a passage from *Ulysses* which recalls David Jones: 'Madam, when comes the storkbird for thee? The air without is impregnated with raindew moisture, life essence celestial, glistening on Dublin stone there under starshiny *collum*.' It is not only this allusive language but the rich strands of popular language in the same few paragraphs, one strand affecting the other sometimes inside a single sentence, that must have seemed like and in fact were the beginning of a new poetry. Joyce in *Ulysses* opened up language in a new way.

Perhaps at this point one ought to discuss what might seem at first like the same deliberate variation of texture, in Pound's *Cantos*. Pound certainly learnt from Joyce, and because the *Cantos* are poetry, one can say of them as of Shakespeare's plays that they express the world as language, their contact with reality is at the level of language, not of *prima facie* subject-matter, although of course the one depends on the other. There are not so very many tones of voice in the *Cantos* and they are not all equally convincing. Nothing in Joyce or in David Jones is better than the best of the *Cantos* but we should consider the whole poem. Pound is an aesthete who treats the world as the material of art; this is implicit in the style of the *Cantos* and closely related to their subject-matter. It is not true of James Joyce, who is always a realist, and still less of David Jones.

A further reservation that ought to be made about the texture of language of the *Cantos* is that Pound's range of language is often not as wide as it looks. Edmund Wilson says very well of *Ulysses* that 'though Joyce almost entirely lacks appetite for violent conflict or vigorous action, his work is prodigiously rich and alive. His force, instead of following a line, expands itself in every dimension (including that of

Time).' We are speaking of language; books are nothing but language; the sense of a rich life, of a static but vigorous and expanding forcefulness is a question of the texture of language. But life and the world also contain action, and a completely contemplative work of art cannot express reality like an epic poem. The addition of further historical and narrative elements, and perhaps the difference between the real international crisis of the 1914 war and the stagnant waters of Edwardian Dublin, may begin to indicate how it could be that *In Parenthesis* should be a work of deeper or more significant realism, that is of more human importance, than the magnificent flawed masterpiece which was its mother crystal. The strongest criticism that Edmund Wilson has to make of *Ulysses* is of a lack of respect for the reader's capacities of attention, and of 'mechanical combinations of elements which fail to coalesce'. It is not unreasonable to remain in doubt about this failure to coalesce in *Ulysses*; at any rate it means nothing as against the liberating rediscovery, which corresponds to the contemporary Cubist discoveries in painting, that by breaking up the texture of language and widely varying its life context, it would be possible for a poet to express the reality of the world in a newly powerful way. That means that the effect of the co-existence of different kinds of language in a poem could be not to diffuse but to concentrate its power as poetry. There is some analogy with the surprising unity of the works of Shakespeare.

Naturally this is not a formula for instant masterpieces. It is not a formula at all, but an *ex post facto* observation in general terms. It is language, the kind and quantity and mass of language that a poet can use and still be genuine, that makes his work authoritative. One crudely stated reason why Shakespeare expresses more of reality is that he uses more English words than other writers. The same question of unity and variety of language arises in other English poets. It is no secret that the language of many of the rising stars of English poetry in the fifties and sixties is purely middle-class, restrained in colouring, smoothly running but rather awkward: the kind of language that I might be speaking now. There are lines in most poems by most of these poets which are interchangeable. The counter-fashion in England for a more open kind of poem with a definite working-class flavour by no means altered the situation. The new poets like the old are confined by their language to a rather limited implicit comprehension of reality. In the unified everyday language of this kind of poetry there is also a lack of sensuous freshness and strangeness: this is not a matter of the lack of verbal gymnastics or of rhetoric, or of any lack of surrealistic somersaults, but there is surely a quality excluded by these levels of language which is close to the essence of poetry; the lack of it is like the lack of problems in philosophy. It is also a fact that even when it has a working-class flavour such a language is not a revolutionary but a conservative force. What makes revolutions and may be their monument is the truth itself. Nothing else is useful. Writers are progressive or reactionary according to the degree of their authenticity and truthfulness; we ought not to accept any other criterion, but in order to use it well we should clear our heads of propaganda. It is more or less possible to know where you stand with a writer simply by considering the texture of his language.

Of course poets are conscious of their limits and impatient of them. Much of the best poetry written recently in England has been solidly based on the genuine salt and life of provincial speech and the authenticity of provincial life. Basil Bunting in his remarkable late poem *Briggflatts* moves between levels of language with an honesty and effectiveness that recall Hardy. He has a secure basis and a wide field of vision: you can see and hear this in his language. It is not only that his shoulder is behind every stroke of the axe, but the fine swing of the axe itself speaks to us immediately in a forgotten, traditional way of speech. Geoffrey Hill is a younger poet, and his language until now has been austere, rigorous and unified; it had the texture of strong canvas. But now in the *Mercian Hymns*, a book very much admired by other poets, the texture of his language has broken open. He has obviously learnt something from David Jones and from Bunting. There is a new breakthrough by Anthony Thwaite, a poet whose language was once almost sedately unified, in *The New Confessions*, another long poem that shows the same influences. Even in this island where nothing ever happens or is likely to happen poetry is struggling out of its wrappings.

There can be no doubt that this is partly because of the invigorating flood of foreign influences and translations. Lowell has been living in England, Berryman is well known, Peter Porter the Australian poet is a less hamstrung and more vigorous intelligence than an English education would produce. In my own lifetime Robert Lowell has made more sense of more of the world than any other poet in English. Among foreign poets the most recent surprises have been Pessoa in Portuguese and Haavikko in Finnish, both suddenly available in excellent and inexpensive translations. Pessoa belongs to a past generation, but Haavikko might almost be writing in the next room; one is tempted to imitate him slavishly. It was heartening to discover in the last few years the strength of East German poetry. There was usually something stray about a good poet in England, as if poetry were a hobby. A fine poet had the same eccentricity as an obscure gardener. The difference in German seems to be the influence of Brecht. Modern German poets are not a single, dogmatic school, but they have in common a severe decency, and a marvellous minimal lyricism first outlined in Brecht's last lyric poems. Their language meshes with the real world and their subject-matter is realities about which few except satiric poets have spoken in the past. If their social responsibility has to western critics an old-fashioned air, so much the worse for us. The triumph of these poets is the impossibility of not taking them seriously. They speak not only with authenticity but with authority.

In English everyone can see a simple diversification of texture in folksongs and popular ballads which fine-art poetry would have ironed out. It would be rather disgusting to call this effect charming; it is naive and attractive, and it expresses the dimensions of real life where unity of tone would suppress them. Take this from 'Haymaking Courtship':

> A soldier walked in the field one day
> to view the flowers that grew so gay,
> he saw a fair maid stripped in her shirt
> as she was raking round yonder hay.

The soldier and the fair maid are traditional figures; their relationship in the song is conventional; 'fair maid' is a formal phrase. The language of the verse is completely direct, realistic country language, except for the second line which belongs to another universe. A word is as much affected by the context of other words, and a phrase by the context of other phrases as a particular colour in one corner of a picture is affected by and affects all the other colours in it. How is it that poetry works, if it is not the transformation of language by its context? How else do you explain the function of the refrain in a folksong? What else is Basho referring to but the subtleties of context when he says *haiku* should be linked by colour, by echo, by aroma?

The texture and the levels of language of a highly sophisticated urban poet like T. S. Eliot can be analysed in the same way. We know

now from the manuscript of *The Waste Land* that Eliot owed some-
thing to Dickens; he refers in the margin to Sloppy in *Our Mutual
Friend*—who used to read the police news aloud—'he do the police in
different voices'. This marginal note occurs against a passage of deli-
berately variegated dialogue put together from phrases of common
language set into a tragic, that is a traditional literary tragic context,
not only by its rhythms but by Ophelia's last words from *Hamlet*. We
are close to Joyce's technique in *Ulysses*, and to the pages Eliot most
admired in *Finnegans Wake*. There is a most interesting analogy to be
drawn between Eliot's apparently rather profound relationship with
Dickens, and Joyce's relationship with nineteenth-century realism
through Flaubert. T. S. Eliot's language consisted of many elements; it
may be that his greatest poetry was written at a point where these ele-
ments had all but fused into a single tone, but not quite. That is the case
in the *Four Quartets*. In the last of these, with its hollowly and harshly
sensuous first section which seems the pure music of conservatism,
'there is no earth smell/Or smell of living thing'. The poem comes to
life in the conversation with the ghost, an extraordinary mixture of
Dantesque and Shakespearean elements, religious and philosophic lan-
guage, and a realism which would seem like a series of sudden intru-
sions if it were not so fused into the language of the poem:

> I met one walking, loitering and hurried
> As if blown towards me like the metal leaves . . .

What a peculiar mixture of formal and realistic elements. My personal
preference is for an earlier stage of Eliot's poetry: the language he
thought appropriate for enunciating wisdom is not by any means un-
convincing, but it does provoke a kind of mistrust that might issue, as
since his death it has done, in malign questions. If the language of poetry
does not correspond in some way to the tensions, the rich distinctive-
ness and the dialectical changes of our apprehension of reality, if it is
not as poetry and as language the expression of what we think reality is
like, what kind of poetry is it? These demands are built into what we
expect of language because they are human demands.

Beware the middle-class tone. Beware the cultured voice. Beware
the sublime overtone. There is a sense in which epic poetry is not sub-
lime, and no realistic poetry can be; in this sense sublimity is a kind of
falsity. The poet may very well mean what he says, but we are still

being imposed on. The 'steer unwilling to the bull's embrace' is a barren heifer that has been messed about with. If we want to know how poetry works we should take a small model; we should closely examine the verse techniques of children's games, we should trace the growth of folksongs through their versions, and try to understand comic poetry: Gay's *Trivia* for example will teach you more about how poetry works than Milton's spectacular and great literary epic, or at least it will teach you more easily, as I want to show later. There is an unnatural appetite for the concrete in the muses of poetry. How else can we explain the qualities as poetry of Shakespeare's language in the mad scenes in *King Lear*? 'Frateretto calls me, and tells me Nero is an angler in the Lake of Darkness. Pray, innocent, and beware the foul fiend.' 'Why this would make a man a man of salt, To use his eyes for garden water-pots, Ay, and laying autumn's dust. I will die bravely, Like a smug bridegroom.' The essential work of poetry is not done by means of either naturalism or sublimity; it is something that can thrive on unevenness of language and can often best be seen working in simple and traditional language.

Perhaps it is labouring the obvious to say so, yet the texture of language in many of the available styles in contemporary English poetry both in Britain and America seems to betray social situations, petrified in the language of poetry, which we ought to try and fight. It is intolerable to make a public analysis of the work of individual living poets in terms of social forces; what we are discussing is a question of the sources of language. Thomas Hardy based the language of his poetry largely on the common speech of a provincial town, and on the tone and atmosphere of folksongs, with their curious strands of heightened language, which means to say traditional and popular poetic language. The language of popular poetry is not plain; it may be grandiose as the decoration of a fairground wooden horse. At the same time he was a realist, in the same sense as Philip Larkin, which means that like Larkin he brought a whole new area of real life and its language under the plough of poetry, and at the same time Hardy was a master of Biblical solemnity and tragic style and an inventor of words. Even today his crabbed, self-consciously limited style is a powerful and liberating source for the language of poetry. The life-giving realism of the war poetry written at the end of the 1914 war was directly related to Sassoon's understanding of the lessons of Thomas Hardy. 'Putting on the agony, putting on the style' is a different matter, and it still afflicts us.

The prim, unified university language we associate with the fifties in England is not a new phenomenon. It follows from the rather linear rhetorical extravagance of the forties. It is ridiculous to attach a fault or a virtue to ten years of poetry, as if one were putting a label on butter, but I think it would be possible to trace the history of style in English poetry: Yeats was no doubt an influence, so was the early Auden, so was Eliot; and I have the impression that aside from Eliot and Pound, native American poetry was relatively unknown in England until the late fifties. It is unlikely to be true that certain kinds of reality were excluded from poetry because they were thought of in so many words as unmanageable in poems, although relatively speaking, English poetry between the *Four Quartets* and *Briggflatts*, with the lonely exception of David Jones, did pursue a more than usually unambitious course. But poetry cannot express the world simply through its subject-matter; poetry differs from other language only in its quality and its concentration: in the behaviour of language under stress, one phrase shatters, another fuses into something stronger, a word at one end of the sentence alters the behaviour of a word at the other. The texture of language in a poem is never completely the same as the texture of language in ordinary life; the moment at which common or individual human demands will alter radically the texture of speech is the moment at which the techniques of poetry have begun to work, even if the physical sign of this so-to-speak chemical change is no more than a repeated or an end-stopped rhythm or a rhyme.

> 'It is Cabestan's heart in the dish.'
> 'It is Cabestan's heart in the dish?
> 'No other taste shall change this.'
>   (Ezra Pound, Canto IV)

We are now at a stage of the development of the English language when we need to return consciously to whatever may be identified as the roots of good English. No one now writes well as a matter of course. I do not personally believe very much in the effect of Puritan theories of plain speaking or even of the Royal Society's ideals of scientific prose on the history of our language; but we need now to look closely into historical questions of that kind. It is useful to look closely at the history of translations of the Bible into English between 1500 and 1700. The traditional literature of dissidence and revolution in England is still virtually unknown and yet Paine for example is better than Burke. The importance of folksongs for the true, inner history of the language is only beginning to be understood. Poetry in the stage of the language that English has now inevitably reached is a learned art. The learning of poets is peculiar, and quite unlike the learning of universities: university learning for all I know may be its worst enemy. It is impossible to construct the language of poetry in advance; the language does not exist independently of the poems. The poetry does not work by rules. A poem is a particular and beautiful behaviour of language: it is less like the notation of music than like a particular performance of certain particular notes on a particular instrument. But the roots of poetry must diversify if poetry is not to die. We have always been used to dealing with the world outside poetry at a certain level of seriousness, and through a diversified dialectic of understanding. Human language must cope with that, and so should poetry, in its fundamental task of reasoning with the elements of the universe.

It matters little what poetry apparently says about the universe, so long as it is not disconcertingly frivolous or in some other way humanly unacceptable. Poetry copes with the universe in the texture and particular quality of the language, and the language as we know by common sense and will forget at our peril as poets, is in the end the creation of the whole people.

> A brackish reach of shoal off Madaket,—
> The sea was still breaking violently and night
> Had steamed into our North Atlantic Fleet, . . .
> (Lowell: 'The Quaker Graveyard in Nantucket')

You know at once with what degree of seriousness you are being addressed. This language is so completely convincing because it is some kind of newly discovered equation that can be verified in the language, a new chemical redistribution of the elements. But in the behaviour of language under tension, a single falsity, the embodiment in any one word of a flaccid or an emotional habit or one might dare to say a spiritual lie, can immediately seem to invalidate the whole passage. It may be that the consciousness of this disastrous possibility, under the external pressure of undigested Freudian analysis and fiercely rigorous literary criticism, operating together as a kind of perpetual system, have created in contemporary poetry a taste for perfection of language which is in fact morbid, another enemy of poetry. We could learn something from the irrationally selective transmission of folksongs about this question. But it may be that contemporary English poetry has been thrown by the daunting achievement of Yeats and Eliot, at least until now. In the same way the eighteenth century was thrown by the magnificent steel-scaled armour of Milton's verse technique. How should they know it was Italian antique armour, and already in Milton's old age irrelevant to English needs? How should they know that the humanity of Pope was the end of a tradition, and not the beginning of one. We must continually and soberly readjust the usefulness to us of great poets.

Perfection of technique cannot really exist, as Eliot pointed out. Even the technical perfection of Robert Lowell's early poems, which of all more or less contemporary poetry is most comparable to the early Milton, has a meaning only within the language world, which I take to be identical with the spiritual world, of those few poems. Lowell after his first poems moved into a freer, morally stronger technique, just as the English language in its poets moved on from the tightness and toughness of Milton to the free-ranging language, the moral liberty, and the personal ease and decency of Pope. The rejection of Pope because of the formality and the apparently courtly quality of his couplets may have been a necessary but a sad mistake in English poetry. Is it that given what happened in English social history, no one has needed so pliable and strong a language since his time? If you judge him by the texture of his language, Pope appears as one of the most modern of all English writers, and satiric poetry appears as a literary form of the greatest potential interest in our time. Satiric poetry, in Shakespeare's comic scenes, in Pope's imitations of Horace, in Hardy's satires of circumstance, in Joyce's *Ulysses*, and above all in the satiric spirit of many English folksongs, is never unrelated to realism in literature. The unproved assumption of all these arguments from the beginning to this point has been that a poet ought to be a realist. Such an assumption can be validated by reasons outside poetry. The language of poetry and everything in a poem must always be validated by life, by reasons outside poetry.

3

HOW MANY KINDS of poetry there are is an empirical question. It is like the more limited question, what kind of poetry do we accept. The scholars most familiar with Aristotle say that he was as empirical as we must be, however rational his preoccupations, and however rigid that system was which Renaissance scholars built on him. But the discoveries of anthropology have opened to us some important truths about poetry; both about human society and about the kind of society in which particular kinds of poetry may be expected to flourish. Consider for example these lines:

> Je te salue, heureuse et profitable Mort,
> Des extrèmes douleurs médécin et confort.

> [I salute you, happy and profitable Death,
> doctor and comfort to extremes of pain.]

It would be showy to offer an analysis when one already knows that they were written by Ronsard, but even not knowing that, one could surely infer the courtliness, the educated stoicism of his society, and the seriousness with which it would take the most elaborate artifice. No doubt something both similar and different could be inferred from Ben Jonson's ode 'Allegorike'.

> Who saith our Times nor have, nor can
> Produce us a blacke Swan?

The sensibility of poets may be quirky, but they know the sensibility they can expect in readers. Across whatever distances, even poets as isolated as Emily Dickinson and Hopkins speak to a sensibility which is expressed as expectation and as underlying moral law in the language of their age. Sobriety and clarity and sensuous crispness differ from one age to another, even though they are moral matters, and so indeed is sober intoxication, and the way they operate in the sensibility of a given age affects the form and marrow of poetry. Poetry is never merely the imitation of models. The ear is as selective as the eye, and the senses are as moral as the intelligence. Indeed three-quarters of the virtues we

43

really admire are those of the senses. The triumph of Cézanne is the morality of the human eye. He satisfies intuitive expectation. A great part of poetry as of painting is a triumph of the intelligent senses. They have an intelligence of their own that reason comes late to analyse.

There is no static 'human nature', unless we are to depart from the ordinary meanings of English; and in the same way there is no natural or original state of man. Primitive societies turn out not to be primitive. The theoretic basis for thinking that they were was colonialism; but the winning society alters the loser even more disastrously than every social observer alters what he observes. And yet if it means anything at all, however tenuous, to speak of a natural state of man, that is of a semi-permanent more or less universal condition of human societies until they reach a particular point of technological development, then it seems that heroic poetry of some kind is natural to human beings, that it collapses under the influence of literacy, that it exists outside the Indo-European family of languages, but that we can more easily discuss it by confining ourselves to the traditions which are closer to us and which we know more about. Within these traditions there is an extraordinary similarity; there are works of great and amazing power in many languages, but the greatest example is undoubtedly Homer. Yet we are only now beginning to know a little about the dark ages of Greece in which the Homeric poems were incubated, and we must argue by analogy about Homer.

There is an important difference between epic poetry and every other kind. Its dependence on an illiterate tradition, its length, and its variability in performance are not the root of the matter. But the performance, the tradition, the massive construction and the social language of a popular, audience-determined, heroic poetry are equivalent to something like the whole mass of the self-knowledge, the self-transmission and the available expression of reality of a complete society. Such a society is itself complete in the sense that it must be as self-sufficient as it can be. Its values and the crisis of its values, since all these societies are in a continuous process of change, are highlighted in epic poetry, and transmitted in a continually altering form. Its institutions and even some of its techniques are dramatized in epic poetry: though it may be doubted whether Lévi-Strauss was right to suppose that epic poetry might in any realistic sense convey a complete culture from one generation to the next. That is an extreme, diagrammatic statement of what function epic poetry might perform only in a confused, inadequate way. No one really learnt how to make tea by hearing Central Asian epics, and what Odysseus says about boat-building is less practical than might appear. But epic poetry is a massive transmission of agreed values and important truths in a memorable form to an assenting audience; it is profoundly popular; to this extent, many of the later diversifications of literature are a substitute, always less adequate generation by generation as the social organization of society diversifies uncontrollably, for epic poetry.

That is not true of all the varieties of poetry. Lyric poetry, work-songs, ritual poetry, and the entire body of what Sir Maurice Bowra studied as *Primitive Song* existed at the same time as developed epic. Many examples suggest it may be older, and that epic narratives are a special development of heroic poetry. Zulu heroic poetry is much closer to primitive song that it is to any epic development. The conditions for the mating of narrative with primitive forms appear to be flexible metre, a musical condition which is hard to pin down, and a popular tradition which seems to involve a vicious circle of argument about which came first. Lyric poetry has a voracious appetite for popular forms of speech, for pre-rhetorical rhetoric and every given tradition of a particular language. But that is true of poetry as such, of all poetry. Language is human speech, and speech is always also some kind of social gesture. Poetry is something said by someone, whether anonymously or personally. The poet is a sort of magician's apprentice, he must intuitively bring under his conscious or subconscious power those mysterious or unanalysed forces whose activity the intensity of the strain he puts on language inevitably awakes. Poetry is a performance. The sense that Hopkins had that his poems were like his appearance at the Last Judgement was justified, with the exception that we may hope God (whether we believe in him or not, let us imagine him) will probe less awkwardly than we do and more mercifully into the moral roots of our lack of skill.

When epic poetry in its highest development in a vital human society was on its last legs, what emerged as a public substitute was the theatre. It may be important to note, since these things are always a process, and part of a longer process, that the moment of this emergence was the heyday of a remarkable humanism, and that in the same years and in the same place architecture, sculpture, and painting had reached a very high point, philosophy was engaged in a life-giving death-struggle with the past, the European tradition of prose-writing was banging on the doors of the womb, there were theories in the air about a wide diversity of subjects, there was a sense of local liberty and victory, and a class struggle which later was to end badly, and the unit of the population of the city of Athens in which these things occurred was more or less equivalent to the audience of the theatre. Of course there was a long preparation. There are nearly as many undeveloped dramatic elements in Greek epic poetry as there are epic elements in the Greek theatre. Like any poet worth his salt, the Athenian dramatic poets took their building-stones wherever they could find them, and we have no longer the means to trace every piece. But the rhythms of their speech and the flexible metrical system they exploited, even the amazing realism (why is realism always amazing?) of which they are capable, had been a long time in preparation.

Greek dramatic poetry includes tragedy, the intensely presented marrow of epic and heroic and traditional and religious values, and comedy, so much more liberated and to my mind at least even more immediately exciting and liberating, but so much shorter-lived. It was shorter-lived in its expression of reality. Political considerations cut the old comedy short. In its beginnings as a developed art it can be seen to be in conflict with the political world, and not long afterwards the political world can be seen to overwhelm it. It was not open to Aristophanes to leave Germany, as Brecht did, and find work in films in Hollywood; still less to return (with money in Switzerland) to Eastern Germany, as Brecht returned.

> Die Vaterstadt, wie find ich sie doch?
> Folgend den Bomberschwärmen
> Komm ich nach Haus.
>   . . . Feuersbrünste
> Gehen dem Sohn voraus.
>
> ('Die Rückkehr' ['The Return'])

[The Fatherland, how do I find it?/Following the bomber swarms,/I come home./. . . Conflagrations/Go before the son.]

Dramatic poetry, and the dramatic art in prose that follows it, which to this day retains some constructive techniques one might be forgiven for calling poetic, is obviously more vast in the reality it can cover than any other sort of poetry except epic. It is fascinating that dramatic poetry on an important scale was re-invented in the Renaissance. The whole of that story deserves to be followed out in every detail, and in particular the liberating incomprehension of classical models and the liberating influences of vernacular languages have the greatest importance for the whole history of the art of poetry. One might almost say that the more classical any of these neo-classic poets is, the worse he is. Shakespeare and Jonson build on a special tradition, and Racine on a quite different tradition, which from a classical point of view is still more perverse. My brother, Professor Anthony Levi, has pointed out the particular relevance of Corneille to the contemporary values of his own world. The dramatic world of Shakespeare, however much we can know of its origins, its wild audience, and its bizarre formalities, is a curiously wide mirror of reality. Perhaps dramatic poetry expresses the real world in a way in which no other poetry except epic poetry can. It is the best substitute for epic.

It is not only poetry, but every art and craft or ritual which expresses reality. When all these means are concentrated in one we may find the greatest concentration of the real world expressed. But in the process of social changes language has become class-divided and so have social forms and literary forms. Poetry continues to invade the theatre, on the whole unnecessarily and ineffectively. The novel, a bastard of theatre and prose history and romance, has established an audience of its own. In the poetry of Eliot there is an attempt to take over the novel at a higher degree of intensity. Thomas Hardy had already carried out a successful rape of the short story. Literary forms are cannibalistic but none of the audiences are universal. What poetry does is to present realities at a high degree of concentration with an economy of verbal means. The economy or the concentration of means has come to characterize poetry as against other verbal arts. Hence the slim volume and a special minimal economy. Eliot quoted to John Hayward the saying of Sherlock Holmes, 'Cut out the poetry, Watson.' 'That,' said Eliot, 'is what I have been trying to do all my life.' I was once walking in the streets of Athens with George Seferis, and an enormous star hung over the end of the road, as liquid, blue, lucid a star as anyone has ever seen. 'You know,' he said, looking at it, 'all my life I have wanted to write some bad poetry.'

There is no reality for which poetry, language, human beings have no appetite. We can recognize reality only by articulating it, a gasp is not enough. I do not myself believe that even thought is independent of language. Therefore sobriety and articulate discourse are among the most important obligations of human beings. Like it or not we are doomed to rationality, and we are equally doomed to those intense experiments which are the crucible and self-crucible of rationality. It can be shown that philosophy feeds on poetry and equally that poetry feeds on philosophy. At the same time what was meant by 'Cut out the poetry, Watson' is true and salutary. There is a poem by César Vallejo which makes the same point.

> Un banquero falsea su balance.
> ¿Con qué cara llorar en el teatro?
>
> Un paria duerme con el pie a la espalda.
> ¿Hablar, después, a nadie de Picasso?
>
> Alguien va en un entierro sollozando.
> ¿Como luego ingresar a la Academia?
>
> Alguien limpia un fusil en su cocina.
> ¿Con qué valor hablar del más allá? . . .
>
> *(Poemas Humanos;* 5 Nov. 1937)

[A banker falsifies his accounts. With what face to weep at the theatre? An outcast sleeps with his foot behind his back. And then talk of Picasso? Someone goes to a burial sobbing. How after that enter the Academy? Someone cleans a rifle in his kitchen. How dare one speak about the beyond?]

Even a normal degree of honesty imposes a certain unpretentious decency on what it is proper to say in a poem. That is the lesson so well learnt by the East German poets who sprang up in the ashes watered by Brecht. There is more than one poem for example not unlike Vallejo's, but more laconic, written recently in Communist Germany, not in Paris in a fever of enthusiasm in 1937 or 1938. There are still rhapsodical forms of speech that can be used, but perhaps not as many as there used to be, and when they are used it is often with irony. There is a suppressed poem about the Red Army published by Brecht in the twenties:

> Und drum: wo immer sie auch warn
> Das ist die Hölle, sagten sie.
> Die Zeit verging. Die letzte Hölle
> War doch die allerletzte Hölle nie . . .
>
> ('Gesang des Soldaten der Roten Armee')

[And so: wherever they went,/it's hell, they said./Time passed. The last hell/was never the very last hell.]

The intensity of love and the intensity of suffering belong to modern poetry, but so does the intensity of emptiness and so does the subtlety of uncertainty. Philip Larkin is a poet of few certainties but he is likely to last and to be valued for an honesty few writers have attained to. That somewhat negative honesty is like the colder water in the sea that surrounds an iceberg of individuality. It may well be that the wish to addict ourselves to more positive or to hysterical poets is self-defeating. Larkin in his poetry retains all the faculties of a human being, he writes like a person awake. What he writes has some relation to a letter or to an entry in a private journal. The modern metaphysical poem can speak of anything, but it has to touch at least by implication on the most serious thoughts and feelings. That is partly because so much weight of significance is put on so few lines. It is not commonly felt decent to call public attention to anything less weighty. On the other hand it is clear enough that it would in fact be humanly decent to do so, and many modern poets have an abounding admiration for the occasional verses of the past. It is the nostalgia for an atmosphere in which poetry would be as natural as breathing. Up to a point this nostalgia is a just wish: the point is that in principle it is more unnatural not to write poems than to write them. But given all this, and adding what each reader understands of the history of poetry, and given that we live as we do, it leads us towards the question: what is poetry for?

That is naturally inseparable from the more empirical question of what poetry does and how it works. In recent times there have been special limits: it is the world that has altered, and the scope of our possible honest relations with it; it is not only poetry. But the result is as if an acid yellow had entered the light of the sun, and it is obscure to the eye whether this chemical fixative belongs to the new conventions of poetry or the newly redefined limits of reality.

> I listen to money singing. It's like looking down
> From long french windows at a provincial town,
> The slums, the canal, the churches ornate and mad
> In the evening sun. It is intensely sad.

(Larkin: 'Money')

It would be disingenuous not to notice that this is profoundly conservative and despairing, profoundly decent and extremely English poetry. Any political criticism would have to take that into account. If you prefer another attitude, see if you can make it sound. Larkin is not a poet who sees many possibilities of change for the better. The East German poets are in an even more terribly fixed situation; something colder than a provincial calm has gripped the very air their poems breathe in. But there is a strange similarity to Larkin about the honesties and the ironies. And for all his salivating after ripe commodities, Wallace Stevens has a spiritual spareness; so has Philippe Jaccottet, for all his quiet lyricism.

> Cris d'oiseaux en novembre, feux des saules, tels sont-ils,
> les signaux qui me conduisent de péril en péril. . . .

('Le combat inégal')

[Bird-cries in November, willow-fires, so they are,/the signals calling me from danger to danger.]

Clearly enough to anyone who reads a lot of it, what poetry now does is to offer a sort of intellectual commentary on life, often slightly superior and slightly impotent in tone. The reality it expresses is one to which the poet's reaction has often been hysterical or numb. It need not necessarily be so, and the greatest examples, including both Larkin and Lowell, have a powerful grip on the real world. But in minor modern poetry the experience may be genuine yet the language is somehow not, and it is nothing but authentic language that can express reality in a poem.

First of all a poet has to be genuine; there is more than one quality for which we can read or praise a writer, and no exact hierarchy exists of all these qualities, but genuineness is the foundation. Genuineness merges into authenticity and authenticity into authority, and authority merges into greatness. Authenticity adds an element of precision and significance to what is genuine; whatever is genuine is acceptable, whatever is authentic is admirable. But authority is something moral and profound. There is no lack of talent, even perhaps of genius; what we need has a moral as well as a social basis. As for greatness, that is something we read backwards into poems or more usually into a poet. It has little to do with any realities except the reality of our own needs. A great poet has done what his own or later or many generations really needed. Greatness so defined has more to do with humanity than with literature. It is not a further degree of an excellence other poets have in a lesser degree, it is a different matter. The size of a great poet is defined by our need for him. At the same time, authority shades off into greatness.

There is another important distinction between the major poets or important poets in a given language and the necessary poets. These last are the poets who, however slight or at a tangent their achievement may be, are the ones you need. Your copy of their poems is falling to bits, you choose them irrationally often for a journey, and it is not only you who need them but the language itself would somehow not look the same without them. In English Henry Vaughan might be such a poet, or Christopher Smart. But the category of necessary poets creates like a shadow a category of unnecessary major writers, the ones there is no particular reason to read, however important they are. It is better to pass over their names in silence as in practice one passes over their books. But what can make a minor poet more interesting than a major one is something human, perhaps something quite outside literature, on which poetry feeds. In this way it is a minimal reflection of what we call greatness, it is enough to attract hunger without offering the profound satisfaction of any common need.

At the gates of modern poetry stand figures like Kavafis, Pessoa, Laforgue, and Trakl. There is something strange about each one of them, and it is an odd phenomenon that modern poetry should have depended on these weird intelligences. The reason presumably is that each one of them was committed to a life-and-death struggle for honesty, for each one of them irony was a weapon close to his hand, and all of them were passionately anxious to break out of that accepted world which may be likened to an over-furnished room. Maybe just as only such a disorientation could reveal the new techniques, so only Marxism, with the shirt of Nessus that Marxists have worn in the last fifty years, could open, as it did in Lukács and in Walter Benjamin, the windows of a new criticism, a new theory. The theory is still incomplete, nor is this book a contribution to it. A theory has to be rigorously worked out by those who accept all the implications, who are willing to live and die by them. What I have to say is more haphazard. If this admission needs to be defended, the defence is that my primary concern is poetry, and poets work intuitively, analysis is secondary. The question of what should be done in the world is a human question, outside poetry. My own belief is that the human possibility of change for the better, and the obligation to courage and the common-sense quality of hope, are close to being absolute and universal; they have the status of moral laws. This is bound to affect any judgement of mine about poetry.

But theories about poetry are only valuable for the poetry that flourishes out of them. It is fair to say that Marxism has been utterly unproductive in Aragon. It could be argued that since he became a communist he has become more and more bourgeois, but whatever happened, he is a lesser poet now than he was in 1940. What are we to say of Paul Celan? We must take the suicide of such a poet seriously, but the poems do not die. Theories about poetry have an after-life. When they have produced whatever poems they can, they may still be useful for the understanding of poetry by hindsight. But even so, non-poetical questions have still always to be asked about these theories, and even about the half-formulated values from which theories might spring. We are right to question the values that underlie the rich poetry of Pound and Eliot as closely as we can. It would for example be an open choice for a poet to prefer to produce a less rich poetry with a better or a more honest theoretical basis, if he thought one was available. We would suspect such a poet because of his poor performance, here again rightly. But what is to be said about the career of a poet of great significance who almost by chance has produced rather little, David Gascoyne? What of his marvellous translations of Hölderlin?

> Adorned with yellow pears
> And with wild roses filled,
> The earth hangs in the lake.
> And wondrous love-intoxicated swans
> In peaceful holy waters dip their heads.
>
> ('The Half of Life')

Here is a poet as interesting in his theories as he has been in his poetry. Most poets throw off their theorizing without a great weight of passion. Auden is so seductive an essayist that one is tempted to take one's eye away from his astonishing talent: but when that talent has full play, it is as much a matter of language, of Auden's inwardness with the English language, as the far stiffer, more puritanical talent of David Gascoyne. The variety and fecundity of Auden and his promiscuity in whoring after every literary form that attracted him throughout a long life, a certain lack of performer's inhibition in him combined with severe technical standards, produced a poet unexampled in modern literature. Eliot and even Pound were less abundant. It is still impossible for me to recall certain lines by Auden without a physical excitement. 'O love, the interest itself in thoughtless heaven . . .' This line offers one of the most longed-for rewards of those who read poetry closely, a new rhythm in a fresh tone of voice.

Ought poetry to be uplifting? It ought at any rate from time to time to be liberating. It can be so in the fresh power of the genuine rhythms of the language, when they are used in some new counterpoint. It can be so in its subject and in its meaning. It should seem to do more than language can by doing with perfect force what language is meant to do, by releasing the energies and purging away the unwanted machinery of the language. Uplifting poetry would have the economy of well-designed metal machinery; in the famous high flights of Dante, the rhetoric and the syntax are economic in exactly this way, and the same can be said for the Latin hymns of Thomas Aquinas, a unique masterpiece of dogmatic language. Sublimity and simplicity are closely related. The poetry is the context of the rhythm. Auden in a few poems and Eliot in as few are perhaps the most inspiring and liberating of modern poets in English. Pound may be as moving and more powerful, but there is something diffused and aesthetic about the heart of his intentions which is hard to accept. But Auden's late wish to be 'a minor Atlantic Goethe' is also bad news. Eliot remains mysterious, and almost more so in his theory than in his practice.

4

WHAT IS POETRY in fact for? What can it do at best, even on the most inflated reckoning? It is hard not to answer such a question rhetorically and inevitable to answer it personally.

When I ask myself about the use of poetry my mind becomes crowded with insubstantial thoughts. One has the sense that poetry is politically good in some Platonic sense of the word political. Poetry is a kind of awakening, both at a certain time of life and perpetually in the case of certain poems: *comme un vin vieux qui rajeunit le sens.* It is a marvellous articulacy of human speech, like the leaves on a tree at an unexpected season, or like some very truthful painting while the paint is still fresh on the canvas. Poetry is poem by poem an attempt to say what every generation has wanted to say and yet no one has been able to until now. Poetry is a kind of secular prophecy, and a kind of more human law-giving, and a kind of more substantial music. The lack of confidence we feel in the theory of poetry seems really to belong to the practice: the trouble is that most modern poets are not good enough: it always seems for one or another given reason impossible at any given moment for someone to write an absolutely convincing poem, one that articulates the deepest truth about our lives and natures, and might live for century after century in the mouths and the understandings of human beings.

Poetry has also a blacker aspect; there is very often a confrontation of death or of chaos held together by the centripetal formal forces of a poem. There is a sense in which good poems are genuinely anarchic: absolutely no external law has in that sense any jurisdiction over the ground of a true poem. Like all human constructions poems have laws of their own: but except for certain marvellous monsters like Yeats for example, and certain passages in Shakespeare, the political colour of the internal laws of poems is frequently of the left; one might say poetry now was at the same time too left-wing to be Christian and too Christian to be left-wing. But this is an external and a foolish observation. The inner logic of poetry is subtle. Still, the death of Lorca was not an accident: people used to say that war is diplomacy continued by other means; and the death and the imprisonment of many poets is poetry continued by other means. But it is the internal law of poetry, which the nature of poetry obscurely but certainly dictates, that will bring us to the heart of this subject. One ought to approach more cautiously.

I suppose for English poetry and perhaps everywhere in the world in the last few years the outlook for poets has appeared particularly bleak. The reasons for this are almost too sad and really too particular to discuss. All our languages have been and are being debauched by a process like the inflation of money; and worse than that, the entire framework of life expressed in ordinary values, that huge unconscious construction which is the life of each language and which if you could see it would be like the expression and the image, the Logos of each human society is being confused and darkened beyond recognition. The entire construction is in fragments. Previously if you wanted to see what your language was, what for example the whole English language really was, you could have seen and understood the whole force and meaning of English in the work of a poet like Shakespeare, and in the old Bible. Fortunately one can still do so. But in our lifetimes the great poets of the modern movement have died and after that mighty thunderstorm the ordinary rainfall of contemporary poetry has a trivial sound: and meanwhile our cultural traditions are withering away.

A poet does not usually embody the mainstream of the language. However subtle or genuine or strong his language may be, he will have an individual style (think say of Thomas Wyatt or Thomas Hardy) and this personal style is really a formula of some kind: if poets had no formula, parody would be impossible, let alone self-parody. Only in the work of some one great poet, perhaps one in every language, Shakespeare or Homer or Dante or possibly Pushkin, the formula that makes a particular kind of poetry possible seems equivalent to the genuine force of the mainstream of the language. Shakespeare's poetry in a special way is native to the English language: the true English Muse was Shakespeare's and she always will be. Even in England the bleak prospect for poetry and poets at present has nothing to do with nostalgia for the Elizabethan age. Nineteenth-century dramatic poetry does seem to embody such a sentiment, but the modern movement has released us from it. Yet poetry does belong to the dead as well as the living: when you write a poem, you are speaking also to the dead.

Language is not and cannot be created by any individual: it is essentially the work of all the human beings in the world, and a given language belongs equally to everyone who speaks it. Language is the most impressive work of man. Law is language, reasoning is language, history is language. Any particular language at any time is the unconscious, half-conscious creation and projection of everyone who speaks that language, however humble or however exalted. We take phrases from the lips of the dead and the anonymous. No language can ever be regulated by an academy; everything in English that is being said, written or read now is the English language now. English speech in its outermost definition is whatever could be said and understood as English. The language is the profoundest expression of the people; and this is often true at a level or in a way very difficult to analyse. It is a traditional, popular set of signs and social gestures, and it bears countless traces of its old users. Shakespeare expresses and seems to understand the English people only because in him the English language itself seems to speak. He uses a wide range of it. He is genuine, authentic, authoritative, and great. We know language is popular: at a trivial level we learn a people by learning any new language, and more profoundly we understand the same truth in the study of the kind of poetry in our own language we can honestly call great. It is possible to reduce the principal problem of poetry, that is the principal problem of poets, to a kind of Bloody Question about modern language: not just rhythms and vocabulary but the living texture and the tones of language. Those distempers of language which are now felt in so many countries, and which have led so many living poets into different kinds of wilderness, must in some way be a profound expression of national life. I am not going to try to demonstrate the dismal situation, and I am not advocating any panacea: I do not suppose that believing in God for example makes any difference. You cannot change the spirits and tendencies of modern English, which is a real, independent, live thing, by adding and subtracting propositions. One must accept that language is a true, unconscious, uncontrolled expression of the whole people: in this way it is the only free act of the whole people; it belongs to a freedom we are unable to tamper with. It may be that modern Greek writers, so unlucky in some ways, have been lucky in another, since the difficult history of modern Greek has forced them to grapple consciously with the problem of language.

It is possible to be more particular. Accepting the fact that a poet works in his own language like a mason in his own stone and a painter in the light of his own sky in his particular century, what really are the uses of poetry now? What use is left for it? In spite of exceptions the proper language of poems is the native language of the poet, and that language is determined by the nation, not by a poet: just in the same way the uses of poetry depend on the kind of poem and the form of speech: but the value of these is determined not by the poet but by the conditions of life in his time. In principle, poetry can do whatever the language can do: a poem is nothing more than someone's particular human speech in which the pressure of rhythm, alliteration and formal repetition have set up a counterpoint between the movement of his thoughts, his own presence and smell and linguistic habits, and a certain iron musical phrasing. A poem can work in any area of life and any area of language. There are excellent poems in English for example about how to cook a lobster and about eating oysters, there is a memorable poem in Latin about a sleepless night on a miserable journey, there are poems about work, psychiatry, the failure to answer letters. I can think of no subject and no popular form of language which is anti-poetic. Indeed the 'antipoetic' has a special value for poetry, as Shakespeare knew. There is an attractive poem of some merit which used to be attributed to Virgil, based on the ordinary Roman form of tavern advertisement. What limits the subject-matter of poetry in a certain period of the world, and defines the kind of poems that are actually written then, has to do with the particular range of speech people feel it appropriate to employ in language so heightened. Once again this has to do with the recognition of a need, a use. If we may exclude games and virtuoso performances, people only need poetry on subjects they care about. The disciplines of verse are a preparation for an explosion, like the ramming of gunpowder into a cannon: but you only fire the cannon on certain occasions: weddings, royal funerals, religious festivals, music by Tchaikovsky, and of course real battles. The kind of occasion determines the kind of poem. What is inscribed in stone and what is expensively engraved take on qualities from their social function. You can almost say the potential poem, the great un-written poem, exists in the unknown need of the audience which is the people, and in the language which is the people, but not in the poet until it exists as words which have left his lips. From that moment of course the poem is not his own, he is nothing more than a confused, distracted member of his own audience: he alters his function and becomes a critic of his poem.

To extend the subject-matter of poetry is not necessarily to alter its use. What alters the use of poetry is the inner form of the poem, the innermost formal purpose, the point at which what a thing is, is the same as what it does. Once the poem exists you cannot reasonably ask what this particular poem is for; you can only ask what it does, what it is. Form is always particular. The form of a poem is not the length of the lines or the physical shape of the poem on the page, it is certainly not identical with any metrical analysis which a future professor may see fit to make of it. It is worth repeating that the notation used for metrical analysis is so inadequate and so selective as to be a downright lie. By the form of poems we mean the profoundest structural element, something that the poet himself may possibly not always grasp before writing, something more concrete than the Petrarchan or anti-Petrarchan sonnet, since no two poems have exactly the same form. It is a semantic pattern in a syntactic husk, and the tone of voice is crucial to it. It might be defined in terms of the social gesture of a given set of words in a given society. More loosely, it is the way a given poem has decided to work at the moment when the Muse smiled and sat back.

But vocabulary, length, and rhythmic elements, and all that side of a poem are a compromise. What the poem is fundamentally doing cannot be compromised, it can only be obscured or muddled. The compromise is between the demands of the language with its particular genius and its particular habits, some of them beautiful, some slovenly, the conventions of poetry, the need for freshness, and the personal emotions and tones of the poet himself. A poet may well feel that how the poem works and what it does arise from the subject-matter of his poetry, and do not belong to him, but surely this is often untrue. The form of the poem comes from the world only by coming from something fundamental in the poet's relation to the world, which he may or may not know or admit. No doubt Solomos, the poet of Greek independence, believed the personal rhythm of his poetry came from the electricity in the air, and he believed he was writing about the national revolution; he believed the revolution dictated what his poems were, and what they did, and yet in fact at one level he was writing a kind of poetry that was not so much Greek as European, and at a deeper level he was writing not national poetry but the purest self-expression. Of course Solomos' achievement is gigantic and truly national, particularly perhaps in his fragmentary poems. But the sources of his poetry were literary and imaginary; he was fuming with fantasies; he has the intelligence of a Greek Adam but the eyes of Narcissus. The extraordinary events of those years, about which the sober truth is so much more impressive that Solomos' heroic fantasies, found their true poetry perhaps in prose, in the memoirs of a man who I suppose was one of the morally noblest human beings of the nineteenth century, the peasant General Makryiannis: and also they found it in a poetry even more extravagant than that of Solomos, and at the same time harder and truer, in some of the anonymous folksongs of that period. The difference is precisely a difference of form in the deepest sense. The people for whom Solomos wrote were imaginary and glittering; his popular success was an imagination come true. That is often what happens when the voice of poetry seems to become the voice of a revolution: it breaks out like a thunder-clap, while the revolution itself smoulders and rattles. The causes of genuine revolution are not imaginary, but the sources of romantic revolutionary poetry are. The inward form of revolutionary poetry of this kind, the social gesture it embodies and the way it works, are not dictated by the circumstances of real revolution. Consider the difference between the words of the 'Marseillaise', which is a fantastical and romantic projection, and the terribly practical words of those songs which the French Revolution really bred: the 'Carmagnole' and 'Ça ira'. Here we are not in the realm of a great poetry, perhaps hardly of poetry at all, but on a far edge of poetry where distinctions become clear. To return towards the most important uses of poetry, I would like to suggest an example, which seems to me to be thoroughly mysterious: the Cretan poem *Erotokritos*.

Its prehistory is very peculiar. Of all the idiotic uses to which poetry has been put—Christmas cracker rhymes, phoney epics, and the scientific verses of Erasmus Darwin—it might reasonably be thought that one of the silliest is the more extravagant verse romances of the middle ages. To read the *Romance of the Rose*, and then to read Dante is like leaving an endless film about a *thé dansant* and walking outside into sunshine. To compare French verse romances with Homer is simply horrifying: one is really shocked at the possibilities of human decadence. The romances are sweet and musical enough in their way, but the need that conjured them up, the need to show off, to smother the world in sugar and to employ that tinkling noise and those woeful erotic overtones 'to lull a drowsy Emperor to sleep', is one of the most appalling indictments of the feudal system. Homeric poetry grew up among a people to whom the values of the *Iliad* and the *Odyssey* were real and critical: it embodies a moment and a generation to which it had suddenly become possible by the use of writing to make out of centuries of true feeling and good tradition, and out of what was essentially performance, the habitual captivation of one particular audience on one particular night, suddenly a mighty poem of enormous length that would live for ever. The *Iliad*, the idea of an *Iliad*, would have been no more possible a hundred years before than it was a hundred years afterwards. The strongest of the various elements in medieval romances is the form of the folkstory which is almost smothered. Yet these poems were popular: people read them. Some of course were better than others. Finally, you might think almost by chance, the tradition of literary, romantic epic which by the sixteenth century had produced scholarly poetry in Italian and pleasant enough stories in all kinds of languages, produced in Crete, that is in the remote province of a backward empire, and in a language and dialect not a scholar in Western Europe could speak, the *Erotokritos*.

It should have died out at once: it should have run to one or two editions, and then been forgotten. If that had happened one may be mournfully certain no scholar would have understood its importance perhaps until this present time. Yet in fact by a popular miracle, this mannered, conventional, extraordinary poem, full of Italian influence and literary artifice, and provincial as it was from a Venetian point of view, through its truly Greek resonance and through the language in which it was written, and through a deeply sympathetic poetic conception, came into use as the national epic of Crete. One should be diffident as a foreigner in speaking about its quality, but anyone who has heard it sung in the Cretan mountains and seen the tears streaming down the faces of the shepherds will understand something serious about the uses of poetry. Its language is strong, sweet, and genuine. But it remains one of the most unexpected events in the history of European poetry that this odd, beautiful poem, which is as artificial in its chivalry and its rhetoric as Yeats' enamelled Byzantine singing-birds, should have been genuinely popular in Crete for over two hundred years. There are still Cretan children, or there were until the last ten years, who knew enormous quantities of it by heart. It suggests at least one new answer to the question 'What is the purpose of poetry?' The purpose of it is to sing your child to sleep with something like the *Erotokritos*. It is the transmission of a language and a criterion. Scholars have demonstrated that it owes more to the traditional language of Greek medieval folksongs than it does on a linguistic level to French or Italian romances. But it will die in popular tradition when Cretan dialect dies.

Every poem must have a starting-point, usually in the language of ordinary life; sometimes a poem has this starting-point not in any of the ordinary forms and phrases that life throws up, but in other poems: this is not necessarily a disadvantage, as the *Erotokritos* demonstrates, and as Shakespeare demonstrated more than once; but in any very long imitative tradition, if only because of the random occurrence of lack of talent, there must surely be a law of diminishing returns. In the end nothing will be left but poetic thoughts about poetic attitudes, which one might well dismiss as hopelessly unreal and unimportant. What is the real need for such a tradition? What has it to do with the expression of reality? It is true that in a world where cultural values have an increasing status as they become more unreal, and old traditions are more available for study, it has become difficult to avoid a stifling waterfall of dead poems and meaningless voices out of the past; it is becoming harder to confront anything real in direct language. The same may well be true of the language of drawing and painting, and the language of photography. There are times when the human race is stammering, when, for reasons outside the analytic powers of any individual, the most important words or any simple significant words become hard to articulate. There is no way out of this. There is no criterion but genuineness, there is no point of departure but experience of life, at which articulate poetry can begin.

Some alleviations are possible of course: by translation, and by the studied enrichment of the native language, a poet can widen, deepen, or make more supple whatever he understands of his tradition. But when the new comes, it will take off like a rocket. It might even be centuries later that some scholar understands the contribution some poet made; that is what happened in the case of Christopher Smart, and very possibly in the case of *Beowulf*. It is worth considering the case of

Dante. If ever the transmutation of metals occurred in poetry, it happens under one's eyes in the *Divina Commedia*. Yet Dante took the classical mythology which is such an effective part of his poems not out of the classical authors he talks about, but out of the most jejune, moralizing bald prose commentaries on Ovid. It is the same thing, on a grander scale, as Keats taking all his mythology out of Lemprière's *Classical Dictionary*. One can see how much Dante took from Provençal poetry, how much in his management of vernacular language he took from Latin, and how much of his poetry was a kind of dream or nightmare about religion and about physical love; and yet there is hardly a poet who had any influence on Dante fit to be compared to him. In a way the whole question of what poetry is for begins with Dante. One might argue that he was the first poet after the introduction of writing to deal absolutely seriously and consistently in his poetry with the most important human issues. Ever since Dante, the peak of poetry has seemed to be committed to those vast questions and cosmic landscapes. They have become the natural stuff of poetry. When you ask what poetry is for, the answer has somehow to reach towards Dante. In his different way, Eliot has done something similar to modern poetry in English. Lucretius and Horace are similar cases.

But the trouble begins when we ask what modern poetry is for. Poetry at any time is the language of that time, including the traditional language of its literature, harnessed and strengthened in a way that people need or want or have a feeling for. The most important poetry in our eyes, since we have read Dante and Coleridge and Eliot, is closely bound up with the expression of the deepest attitudes of this age in its most characteristic language. If therefore we are to ask what poetry does now, or what social function there is for poetry, we shall have this at the back of our heads. We shall be sure that in the disguise of some reduced or some new social function, poetry will be doing its old work, which is like the work of the sea. But I am not sure that we shall be right. Poetry is a kind of possibility, it is there if someone wants it or feels the need for it; but it is also a tradition; poets learn from other poets, and poetry now, with some few exceptions, is written to be printed in small volumes for educated people of eccentric sensibility. In England if not in America there are poems still being written to be bought by a very genteel, respectable class of people. I remember the barmaid in one of the London theatres where Eliot's plays were shown, saying to a friend of mine, 'I do like Mr Eliot's plays, of course I don't look at them but you get a nicer class of people.' There is another kind of poetry which belongs first and foremost to young people; in his time, which is not yesterday, that was the position of Auden. There is a third kind of poetry which is simply popular: it belongs to the world of peace movements and marches and the revival of folksongs.

There is what might possibly be defined as a fourth kind of poetry, a sort of public poetry, written to be recited, with a definite clear message for which the poetry provides nothing but a metallic noise. This kind of poetry, which interests theoretical writers very much because of a close relation to a real social need and a living audience, is likely to be political, or satirical, or occasional. It may be worth under-lining that there are certain kinds of poetry which are no longer written. Poetry does not always inevitably continue to work in the same way. It is at least as Protean as the language we speak.

Yet the uses of poetry recur in the history of mankind: an old use loses its meaning, but it often reappears long afterwards. The political poetry of the early Greeks had a function which died out because of political changes, yet the political poetry of Pope in English has some-thing like the same use: and in the poetry of Yevtushenko for example, and the whole strong Russian tradition in this century of serious and public political poetry, the similarity to the Greeks is even closer. Propertius in Latin was a learned poet writing about love, hoping to be read by young girls and young men who were not particularly respec-table: he nourished his wonderful poems on popular love-magic and who knows what else: a sub-literary culture as plaintive as jazz. Long afterwards and quite suddenly the poetry of Wyatt is as witty and as passionate and as free of illusion.

> They fle from me that sometyme did me seke
> With naked fote stalking in my chambre . . .

It has been a mistake to try and reduce poetry to only those functions that nothing else can fulfil. Poetry is a vast area, and it includes limericks, obscene verses, public hymns, philosophy; anything that can be said by human beings can be said best in a poem. Even naturalistic imitation is possible in poetry. There is no one message or one kind of message we should expect poets to transmit in poems. One model of poem, the rather difficult, metaphysical structure which proposes important truths about life and the universe, has become an obsession since the break-down of systematic religion. We have even come to expect a kind of apocalypse from poetry, so that there exists now also an alternative tradition of poets whose only message is that poetry has no apocalypse to offer. Every poetic form produces at the same time its opposite. 'My mistress' eyes are nothing like the sun' is an early example. There is an earlier and surely an unacceptable example in *The Parliament of Fowls*, where Chaucer produces a cloying inversion of the inscription on Dante's gate of hell. Poems about ultimates will continue to be written, because the moral expectation aroused by poetry cries out for the straight confrontation of an important issue. But the best poems about ultimates have also another dimension; there is the sense that in them the language itself is confronting the whole of life. Of course the poetry is particular. There is always a unique answer to the question of what even one line of poetry is and does.

Compare for dramatic excitement any one of the entry lines in Shakespeare where a place is mentioned by name with the opening words of Marlowe's *Tamburlaine*: 'Now hang our bloody banners by Damascus.' There is a long list of these dramatic lines, they all belong to awe-inspiring plays about great historical events, and they all contain an element of horror or doom, but of course they are all completely different. Or take the last words of Brutus in Shakespeare's *Julius Caesar*:

> Night hangs upon mine eyes; my bones would rest.
> They have but laboured to attain this hour.

There are lines of this kind throughout Shakespearean tragedy and down to the time of Dryden's *All for Love*. The differences are very great but there is always some sense of a profound level of the language. There are universal elements in human experience which creep into the poet's voice. There is a natural law that poetry, just because it is the ordinary language of life under tension, shall be a kind of echo-chamber for these elements. During the writing of a poem the difficulty the poet has is to keep out such echoes when they are unwanted. The discipline of poetry is suppression of the overtones and implications of tense language whenever there is no good reason to give them free play. The greater the degree of tension put on human language, the more likely it is to be humming in sublime undertones. Sometimes they can be compacted into a significant pattern. But as often as not a poet may wish to be rid of them. They are a pseudo-religious mummery, like bardic robes. Jean Cocteau once said that the dream of poets is not to be admired but to be believed. No one believes a man in bardic robes.

The internal laws of poetry work like this. First the human being who is writing a poem is subject to every human law which is buried in the uses of human language: the laws of reason itself, because even the subtlest intuitive perceptions and even the most mysterious religious truths, once they exist in words are inevitably subject to reasoning: the laws of reason are also laws of language. Then, the person who is writing a poem is subject always to a greater demand for clarity, truth, and exactness, otherwise the sublime undertones and the silly atmospheric noises of his poem will destroy it. He is subject to certain laws of art which always take the form that you cannot have one thing without sacrificing another: but of course these laws are empirical, and cannot be precisely stated even on the basis of great experience. The last and most interesting internal law of poems is moral. There is a logic about this; a poet who behaves less than well in his poem, that is less than decently as a human being, will ruin his poem; but the better his poetry becomes, the profounder and the greater discipline his own poems will impose on him. This lies at the root of the human greatness of great poets. Their goodness is that of a good piece of wood, or they are good in the way in which water is good. The continual expression of reality in speech requires great honesty and courage.

If it is permitted to speak even more wildly than I have already spoken, there are three apparently permanent functions of poetry, all secular but all in a sense prophetic, which I would like to point out. One is to instil or to insinuate goodness. That is what Aristophanes thought was the duty of poets. 'We must say really excellent things, because little boys are taught by schoolmasters, but adolescents listen to the poets.' For an example of a poet instilling goodness, I would choose Pope's *Epistles* or Horace's *Epistles*. A second important function of poetry is to be articulate about death. The obvious examples are almost too many. This is the subject-matter of many ballads and of the *Iliad*. It is the subject of the most terrible and direct of all Latin hymns, maybe of all medieval poems, the 'Dies Irae'. And thirdly there is a mysterious use of poetry which shadow-plays the return of human beings to their first justice, the vindication of mankind, the renaissance of antiquity, the resurrection of the dead. It is no more possible to exhaust this use of poems by verbal analysis than it is to pin down the psychological functions of mythology, to which of course I am referring. There is an excellent and strange example in Shakespeare's *Pericles, Prince of Tyre*, in Act Three, Scene Two: the opening of the chest.

And yet it would be intolerable to conclude on so high a note. The bias of poetry for the concrete is an internal impetus in every formal context. What poetry is for is to present human speech honestly, and if a poem can be honest and concrete it is worth more than the highest aspirations or the most mind-boggling mythology. I would surrender a few lines even from the works of Shakespeare for Heinz Kahlau's old bricklayer: 'Begrabt ihn ohne Lügen.' ['Bury him without lies.'] The slightest rhythm that catches a tone may express more of reality than a laborious treatment of great themes. It is positively misleading to ask questions about poetry and answer them always in terms of great poetry, or still worse, sublime poetry.

> Maigre immortalité noire et dorée,
> Consolatrice affreusement laurée . . .
>
> (Valéry: 'Le cimetière marin')

[Thin immortality, black and gilded,/consoler with the terrible laurels.]

These two lines may well be less useful for an enquiry into the nature or purpose of poetry than the simpler, less impressive lines of an old popular song. What most people most value in poetry is that some few lines of a poem catch a human tone. In fact the tone of voice of a poet, which is immediately identifiable as his, tells us at once how seriously to take him. In the first four lines of Peter Huchel's 'Der Garten des Theophrast' there is a tone of voice entirely his own and yet belonging to this one poem. It is not just his being at ease in the rhythms of his language, or the moving quality of what is said; there is also something particularly serious and compelling about Peter Huchel's tone of voice. Language is social gesture and we can hardly fail to recognize tones, even in a dead or a foreign language.

> Wenn mittags das weisse Feuer
> Der Verse über den Urnen tanzt,
> Gedenke, mein Sohn. Gedenke derer,
> Die einst Gespräche wie Bäume gepflanzt.
> Tot ist der Garten, mein Atem wird schwerer . . .

[When at midday the white fire/of verses dances above the urns,/consider, my son. Consider those/who once planted conversations like trees./
The garden is dead, my breathing gets more difficult . . .]

This tone of voice may often provide an entry into the work of a poet who is puzzling or to poems whose attraction it is difficult to analyse. The power of poetry is a power of context and the tone of poems is a crucial part of that. A personal tone is a sort of audible hand-writing. In the life-work of a poet one can see the power of context building up in sequences and in a great mass of poems, and everything that comes to have special resonance in a life-work helps towards a clear reading of the tone of the poet. The way the context works in a poem, the way it comes to bear, depends on tone, and is recorded as tone. The personal tone of a poet can be parodied but never successfully imitated. It arises from the intuitive expression of what is most personal in the man, and from inaccessible laws that are present in the bones of the language. It is like a personal style of habitual social gestures. The tone of voice of such a poet as George Seferis or Osip Mandelshtam, to name two highly distinctive poets, or in English Eliot, is immediately riveting to the attention. There is something very serious and very complicated about it. It obeys the important rule that poetry now has to be at least as serious and as resourceful as modern prose. At the same time these tones are not eccentric, they are curiously close to the bone of the language. It might be important that the prose writings of Seferis, as of Eliot, and in his way Mandelshtam, were individual and very impressive.

It is in this relation of personality and selection to the deep structure of the language itself that the genius of poetry consists. Language is always learnt, always common, always habitual. A personal feeling for it is an intuitive selection of what is genuine, or flourishing. It entails an intuitive moral or socio-moral reading of everything one might say. There is no appeal except to the language itself, there is no final decision except the slow judgement of generations of the people who speak the language. In recent times there has been in England and perhaps also in the United States a tendency to value as genuine whatever is popular, whatever has local provincial roots. This is surely not the same as the bone or marrow of the language; its chief advantage is that it breaks away from smoothness. But Auden's eccentric habit of collecting lists of rare words out of the dictionary and then deliberately using them seems even further from a true understanding, such as in fact Auden often otherwise showed, of how the language works.

Even without moving between different social levels of speech, a poet may alter and deepen his tone continually even inside the walls of one poem, by a process of breaking himself up, a self-criticism of his own language. Wyatt's 'They fle from me' may be such a poem. Theodore Roethke's 'In a Dark Time', and several other poems in the same late sequence, show the same.

> In a dark time, the eye begins to see,
> I meet my shadow in the deepening shade;
> I hear my echo in the echoing weed—
> A lord of nature weeping to a tree.
> I live between the heron and the wren,
> Beasts of the hill and serpents of the den.
>
> What's madness but nobility of soul
> At odds with circumstance? The day's on fire!
> I know the purity of pure despair,
> My shadow pinned against a sweating wall.
> That place among the rocks—is it a cave,
> Or winding path? The edge is what I have.
>
> A steady storm of correspondences! . . .

How the tone deepens and darkens, how traditionally strong and yet how uncluttered the language is, how the rhythms develop and extend themselves within so strict a metre. Shakespeare is not far away, and yet he is never close enough to disturb the directness of what is said. Roethke has taken a tone as well as a technical knowledge from a much older period, and it is clear he could not have used it in any way but falsely until he really needed it. Few writers write or ever need to write at such a pressure. Poets discover what they need; Ginsberg and Corso learnt lessons from Whitman that had been lying so far as I know unused, and Lowell learnt something from Allen Tate others had not bothered to learn. There is good evidence that Euripides late in his life learnt from Aeschylus, whom Sophocles had not much imitated. The notebooks of Brecht show that he was anxious to learn as much as possible from Kipling.

Another achievement of individual poets that carries a less subtle but an equally unmistakable signature with their tone of voice is their characteristic line. One would not mistake a line of Shakespeare, or of Marlowe, or of Milton, or of the early Robert Lowell. Such a line may be a considerable achievement. It may be analysed metrically and may represent, as Marlowe's version of Ovid does, an enormous improvement in metrical mastery, but such a line is at the same time as personal as breath, it is not a mathematical construction. The Roman satirist Juvenal has no overwhelming virtues at all as a poet except his characteristic line, which is as vigorous as it could be without being discordant. Lowell has translated some Juvenal, and most fortunately for the result it is on the characteristic qualities of Juvenal's line that he has concentrated. It is the best of what Juvenal has to offer; the translation is stunning and numbing and black and disjointed in the same way as the original.

There is necessarily something physical about this discussion. Everything about poems except the physical details of what they sound like is simply too vague, and too untechnical, to tell us much about the nature of poetry. It is probable enough that the greatest modern changes in English poetry, the introduction of free verse and the new deliberate counterpoint of classical short and long against the stress accent, which occurred also in France, depend on an uncontrollable physical change in the language. It is apparently a view shared by many philologists, though I supposed until recently I had arrived at it greatly daring on my own, that English has been altering from a stress-accented language in which pitch is free to be used expressively, to a language based not on stress but on a distinction between long and short syllables. If that should be true, then much of the verse technique of the modern movement in English, as opposed for example to Chesterton's 'Lepanto', is simply a rationalization of the tonal values poets were already actually hearing in the language. It would be fascinating to know whether the influence of French on Eliot and Pound is more or less important than their breeding in American rather than insular English.

Who is it who knows a language best? It is not a question of educated appreciations, though it may be supposed that Professor Higgins in Shaw's *Pygmalion* knew English very well. The knowledge has to be intuitive and may be a crusty and ignorant kind of knowledge. It is almost never attainable by the same individual in more languages than one. The experience of life, and apparently particularly of childhood, in a place where the language is alive, is important. It is necessary that some strains of extension should be put on the language: there ought to be nothing a person is unable to talk about. Someone who knew the language well might probably know a lot of proverbs. He would certainly have an intuitive familiarity with many traditional ways of speech, but without relying heavily on any particular bag of tricks. A poet of any authority would probably have to be such a person. The authority of his poems may be embodied in something as tenuous as a tone, it may be nailed in memory by something as fluid as a line, but what it depends on is nothing but his inward grasp of the language and his technical performance in verse.

5

ALTHOUGH EACH OF US defines what we mean by poetry through the poems we happen to have heard or read, poetry yet makes a similar, or at least a related set of noises in all languages. The best formal studies of these noises are by Roman Jakobson, but there is still plenty to say. There are no languages, so far as I know, and no human societies have been discovered that I have ever heard of, without some kind of poetry. Poetry is not invented, it is not learnt, though it may be relearnt and deeply influenced in one culture from another. Poetry is as natural as language itself. The margins of poetry and prose are sometimes hard to determine, particularly in a society without writing, and in those periods and those societies in which writing is a new thing. There is said to be a Polynesian language in which poetry and prose are indistinguishable except by the circumstances of performance. If you recognize poetry by the noises it makes, you may often be confused even in less eccentric languages by archaic prose. There are in fact a number of languages which at first hearing sound as if everything in them was poetry. But the poetry in a given language, leaving aside the difficult Polynesians, is always in a special relation to the rest of that particular language.

The difference between written and unwritten languages is crucial. Written prose is not the same as spoken language. Prose is subject to the inherent rules of rhetoric. When prose is written it is self-critical and self-conscious, as is poetry, and they define themselves against each other. Prose withdraws from many of the devices of poets, and poetry gradually abandons a wider area of reality to prose. Of course at a later stage of written literature these movements can be controlled and even reversed. John of the Cross as a poet recaptured mystical theology, Milton did his best with the Bible, Alexander Pope made inroads on philosophy and politics, T. S. Eliot in *The Waste Land* invaded what had become the special areas of the novel. Lawrence Durrell, in this not unlike John of the Cross, tried at one time to do in prose what he had already done better in poems. But in any unwritten language all the devices, the subject-matter, the rhythms, and the special noises of poetry already exist in a confused state: these are not the *disiecti membra poetae*, they are the foundations of all poetry and prose in the language itself.

The devices of poetry are not quite the same in all languages or in all traditions. Even without our speaking falsely in Europe of any shared classical or supposed Christian background, which would be very hard to trace, the overshadowing light of the Renaissance gives us an illusion of a greater similarity in fact than the poetries of different languages need necessarily have. I doubt the possibility of understanding the formal devices of poetry transmitted in the Renaissance without knowledge of Hebrew and of Arabic medieval poetry. But European poetry as we commonly know it is sufficiently dense, sufficiently abundant and complicated, to furnish enough materials for an introductory study of what is in common in the noises poetry makes. Trial excavations in non-European traditions seem to me to confirm this view. It is not a complacent Europeanism, but there are social and historical reasons why European poetry in its extent and history contains many different elements. The range of peoples was diverse, the languages were mostly written down early, the choice of models was comparatively vast even four hundred years before Christ. In Palermo in the eleventh century AD the grave-stone of the mother of a Norman priest might be competently inscribed in Arabic, Hebrew, church Latin, and Byzantine Greek. There is no moment we know of in the history of Europe when things were not sufficiently complicated. It is like the history of the Indian sub-continent, where there is still unwritten poetry in scarcely recorded languages.

If poetry is natural and universal, arising inside every language, and if there are many languages inside which we know how poetry behaves, then it ought not to be hard to say what poetry is. Roughly we recognize it by the noise it makes. We also know what given language is being spoken by a typical set of noises, word-formations, and tones, and we can know this in a living language down to the details of a local pronunciation. We can even tell, though less easily without knowing the language, the individual habitual voice of any given person. The grain of an individual voice can be described in words, but not defined in them. What is more, at least in the case of the poets of written poetry, that is of self-critical, consciously formed individual styles, we can often tell the author of a poem simply by the habitual tone of his language: partly that is by the habitual noise he makes, even if we have never heard his voice. The voice of Shakespeare in his poetry is even more distinctive than the voice of Eliot. The same is probably not true of an unwritten or a newly written language. The anonymity of ballads, and the problems of Homeric authorship are a matter of common style, not just of our bad luck in lacking evidence.

Within these limits, it is important that poetry can be recognized in every language in the same way. In every poem the language is put under the physical tension of a rhythm which is not identical with the conventional, or if you prefer it the natural rhythms of that language. Almost always the rhythm is repeated and becomes clearly recognizable to the ear.

> Dark, dark my light, and darker my desire.
> My soul, like some heat-maddened summer fly, . . .
> (Roethke: 'In a Dark Time')

These formal rhythms can be repeated from one poem to another, even from one language to another. The poetry of John of the Cross would be impossible without the fresh impact of the introduction of Italian Renaissance metres into Spanish. Goethe could write in a version of the metres of classical Latin. The iambic pentameter in English was freshly rediscovered, almost certainly under the influence of Latin, in the lifetime of Marlowe and Shakespeare. These empty forms take on a new life in every language they invade, because if the formal rhythm is the same but the spoken, everyday rhythms of two given languages are different, the same formal rhythm produces a different kind of poetry. A Russian poet reciting 'The Ballad of Reading Gaol' in Russian sounds very unlike Oscar Wilde.

Every rhythm creates an expectation of the fulfilment of that rhythm: most obviously so when the rhythm is repeated. It would be worthwhile to explore what kind of expectation a given rhythm may set up, and what kind of poetry it may give rise to, what kind of opportunity it creates for a poet. Here having rushed in like a fool I must pretend to tread carefully like an angel. We know what a formal rhythm can do only when we see what it has done. No one can predict: only the poet himself, under whatever public or private pressure, can see the opportunity in a given rhythm in his native language at a certain time. We should confine ourselves to what we know has actually happened, but in doing so we become blind to some other

possibility of the same rhythm, which a new poet with fresh material
will see when you and I are forgotten. Anglo-Saxon alliterative verse
looked as if it had died with Langland. But Hopkins saw a new possi-
bility in it, Dylan Thomas another. Auden another. And who wrote:

> Sempiternal though sodden towards sundown, . . .
> When the short day is brightest, with frost and fire,
> The brief sun flames the ice . . .

Metrical studies have a limited but exact finesse, yet they are blind, and
always a little awkward.

We ought to clear two problems out of the way. One is the boring
distinction between verse and poetry: I believe this is a social judge-
ment, a class judgement, it has to do with a contempt or a guilty long-
ing for popular speech and low language which is typical of advanced
bourgeois society, and it has little or no technical basis. The other is
more important, and may lead us further into the meaning and behav-
iour of poetic form. It is the question whether poetry has a special
subject-matter. No modern poet worth his salt thinks it has, most
people are sure it has, most modern poetry is distasteful or meaningless
to most people. Surely the solution is that the expectation raised by
repeated rhythm is a certain intensity, or a certain density, equal to the
limits of the form. It involves an inevitable clang of a bell, a strong
closure. It can easily be filled out as a heightening of language in its
antiquity, in its integrity of reason, in its sonority. A poet who raises a
ghost he is unable to lay is lost. He must carry through his rhythm.
And all this helps to determine the subject-matter of poems in a given
society. What is said has to be important. What sounds important has
to be at some level serious. Comic poetry is a paradox of rhythm. The
most powerful passages of tragic poetry are terribly simple. In a class-
divided society the poet is typically expected to be a fresh and modern
Wordsworth. He is to justify society by his independence and sub-
limity. He will not easily be forgiven for betraying that trust. The
foundation of this false role of the poet is the expectation raised by the
noise that poetry makes, the vocabulary and the rhythm. Poetry died
maybe before Christ when it became literature; it certainly died a
deeper death whenever it was that literature became culture. We shall
return therefore to the more cheerful subject of the noise it makes.

I have already said that I think it is impossible in principle—anyway

it is not practicable—to give a complete description of the noise made
by a line of poetry. The meaning is part of the way we hear the noise.
In the classical system, the length or shortness of syllables is funda-
mental, but there was also a beat accent, and the two never corresponded
exactly. In the European system the beat is fundamental, but still the
two never correspond. This sets up a descant. The natural rhythm of
the spoken language, that is the rhythm of syntax, of meaning, also
never or nearly never coincides with the metrical units even for a single
line. When it does so, it produces the gigantic clang of a final closure.
Even a near-perfect correspondence makes a very clear pattern; this is
often used to establish a ground-rhythm. But sometimes the ground-
rhythm is very obscurely established; in that case the moment it
becomes clear is an important and a tense one. Take an example which
establishes this and also another point, that rhyme and half-rhyme are
only two among the many devices that affect a repeated rhythm.

> Yet once more, O ye laurels, and once more
> Ye myrtles brown, with ivy never sere,
> I come to pluck your berries harsh and crude,
> And with forced fingers rude
> Shatter your leaves before the mellowing year.
>
> (Milton: 'Lycidas')

It is not very dignified to pull these lines apart, and it is not possible
to give any exhaustive description of the way we hear the noise they
make. Does the first line establish a minimal unit? Surely it already
establishes the rhythm of classical bucolic poetry, and it also establishes
the voice and tone of Milton, but the line is not end-stopped; maybe
two lines together make up the unit: *more . . . more . . . sere.* The third
line is a near-perfect correspondence of the rhythms of English, dictated
by meaning, with the pentameter, and even though quantity and stress
do not coincide this is a tough line, with a very definite rhythm. Are the
berries harsh and crude, or the line? *Crude* rhymes with *rude*, which
holds back the rhythm yet again, being a trimeter, and the fifth line
fulfils expectation without any hammer-stroke, because even the beat
rhythm is only in descant with the sense that we have by now of an
iambic pentameter. *Year* recalls *sere* and *more*, but there is nothing
softer than a half-rhyme. The word *mellowing* is not a dissyllable, and

it quite alters the rhythm. Substitute *dying* and see what noise it makes. I want to demonstrate nothing about this line except that technical terms do not exist in which we can exhaustively describe it. Therefore we ought to distrust the study of metre, though we ought to be conscious that Milton was conscious of it. But his poetry is as complicated and simple as a waterfall. Even in a lesser poet the length and shortness of syllables are not easy to categorize, nor is the power of a beat. Is it the same on *shatter* as it is on *laurels*? Metre is not a geometric scheme, but a progression of sound. The momentum measures itself and echoes itself.

If the noise that poems make is so complicated how can we study it? Literary criticism is not an exact science. We can hear what we are not able to express or to teach. One poet learns from another by ear, not by theory. A new theory can make a poem sound different, but there are few theories first proposed by literary critics which really influence poets. In the early days of Beat poetry in America, Anselm Hollo I think it was found a beat line in Shakespeare: 'Let me not to the marriage of true minds admit impediment.' That is a poet's insight, not a professor's. It is our privilege as non-scientists that what we can hear we can understand, even if we are unable to describe it, let alone to exhaust it in description. If we study poetry, then even as professionals essentially we are amateurs. We should begin with the noise of the simplest poems, ballads, children's verses, lovers' rhymes, and such a simple form as the limerick. We might find here in simple elements, more easily than in Milton, what expectation, independently of literary tradition, a rhythmic form imposes on the language.

Take for example the ballads in Castilian Spanish, preserved and rewritten among Sephardic Jewish communities in exile from Spain, which are usually older than similar ballads recovered from Spain itself, and which were first printed in Hebrew type.

> Tomo tacsim en su boca,
> y empezo a cantar.

[He took music in his mouth,/and began to sing.]

First of all they introduce the element of music, which cannot any longer be kept out of this discussion. Certain syllables, particularly final ones, are obviously prolonged in music. The strength of the lines also has to do with performance; words are isolated, they must carry a force of emotion. Syntactic pattern has to be clear, but narrative pattern could hardly matter less. The ballads are obscure. They are heard, felt, not read. The sound pattern has to be strong.

> Tres hijos chicos tengo
> lloran y demandan pan.

[I have three young children,/they weep and ask for bread.]

The inconsequence of the narrative is what makes these sudden, strongly-felt lines so moving. The songs were confused before they were written down. But in the written poetry of Lorca the same conditions produce the same qualities. What Lorca was the first to understand is that the form of poems like these and the integrity of life and language that went with them could be heard. The translations of Lorca into modern Greek by Nikos Gatsos confirm the same lesson. In English it is possible that it has still to be learnt.

Lorca was not a professor, the motive was not literary. A poet of any importance is fighting for his life, his passion is for reality. He can say what his language can say, and anything that prose can say poetry can say more intensely. Lorca uses the form he uses because he smells out what it can do. The English form of ballad is more relaxed, more diversified, more spontaneous, usually less strong. The reason for this difference of form is probably musical, in the convenience of a formal repeated line for spontaneous composition. The verse forms that are useful for long narratives are very pliable and variable. The ideal example is the Greek hexameter, but English ballad-verse can do in a lesser degree the same things, and the music which goes with that verse, which can certainly be improvised, since I have heard it improvised with no instrumental music for an hour on end in endless variations, can be traced right across Europe. Unfortunately the more capable and multiform a kind of verse is, the less it can tell us about how the tension that repeated rhythm imposes on poetry works.

The form of children's verses is usually very simple. They are like work-songs, but closer somehow to the marrow of poetry, less obviously dark, more innocent and closer to unreason and to dreams. We are all children and we must all die.

In the North
a long way off
the donkey's got
the whooping-cough...

Sally go round the sun, Sally,
Sally go round the moon,
Sally go round an omnibus
on a Sunday afternoon.

We hear what we are incapable of describing, even in such simple examples. The hollowness and sadness of these poems is emphasized by the curious meaningless meanings, by the isolated sense they make, but it is implicit in the rhythm, and the incapability, whether psychological or technical, of fulfilling that rhythm: 'North—off—whooping cough', 'sun—moon—afternoon'. Tragedy is more terrible; Lear's 'O, O, O, O, O', which fills a pentameter, is more terrible. 'Lloran y demandan pan' may be stronger than a children's rhyme but it is not sadder.

The master of the limerick in English is Edward Lear. He was the saddest of men, for personal reasons, and he wrote his poems almost all for children. They have the same sadness. But the form of his limerick reveals a vital fact about rhythm. He repeats his first line or at least its closing rhyme as the last line. This habit produces a fearful diminuendo which is close to self-mockery and very typical of Lear personally. The noise his poetry makes awakes an unfulfillable expectation. But if you destroy his classic form, which has I believe a remote origin in sixteenth-century Italian, and substitute a fresh rhyme in the last line, the momentum of the rhythm is utterly different, it ends on a dominant note. By that one stroke you produce such a crescendo that no solemn poet has been able to fill it out, and the new form has become the pickings of obscene humorists. The 'old man of Thermopylae, who could never do anything properly' owes his existence to a diminuendo. The 'old man of Madras, whose balls were made of brass', owes his existence to a crescendo.

These simple examples teach us something, but not much. If you know the tune of a song, a suitable general sense will infallibly suggest itself, and the formal patterns of poetry work in the same way. But the same simple point of view may help with more complicated problems.

The combination of a robust rhythm of the spoken language in Thomas Hardy with certain dying falls of versification produce a peculiar quality which personally I value highly. The noise made by his poems is not like any other in English; there is some analogy with Kavafis in Greek, but this is not the place to work it out. The sound of certain lyric poems by Brecht is quite idiosyncratic, but the building-bricks of these poems are as simple as children's verse, and they can be understood in the same way. If one is trying to understand not poems but a poet, then his failures are equally interesting. The weakness can always be detected in the noise the poems make. The magniloquence of one poet, the militarism of another, the lunatic and perverted enthusiasm of a third—it seems invidious to name names—can all be heard in the failure of certain formal devices, in the relation of the noise of the poems to the language itself. Who knows the language, or how do we know the language? By this we stand or fall, as poets, as readers, as critics, as every damn thing: as human beings, as a society. Can you tell there is something phoney about Yeats? Is there anything phoney about Yeats? 'Cut off an ignorant farmer's ears.' 'And one was drowned in the great bog of Cloone.' Is it the meaning or is it the noise? Or are these lines all right? Do they ring right, like bronze or porcelain?

There are no general criteria for what poetry should do or be or sound like. Poetry can be or say whatever the language can be or say; it is the expectation it raises and the basic human principle of economy of means that demand a certain intensity; therefore we judge a poem according to the expectation it raises. Economy of means includes using the means fully, catching the form by the bone. When language is heightened by repeated rhythm every falsity of phrasing is evident and offensive. In reading or in hearing a poem we are judges, but the law is the language itself. There is something moral about craftsmanship. If what can be called social is moral, if there is anything moral in social history, there is a morality about the way we speak. Language is social and it has social laws. The special noise of poetry is what makes it poetry, but that noise is a human behaviour, because all our language is a kind of behaviour. The language is common, speech is individual. No scientific analysis of a poem can be made, because no inhuman, impersonal analysis of individual behaviour will ever be completely adequate. But poetry is a procedure of reasoning, and the laws of every language include always the universal laws of reason. Poetry is subject to those laws. The noise of poetry makes it a powerful language, but a poem is vulnerable; it can easily be seen to fail. The languages of human beings are a severe criterion for the behaviour of poets in those languages.

The noise itself, the special form, is no kind of criterion. Every noise is useful in the right context of noises, and what the form does is to impose such a context. Given the laziness of the human ear, the most conservative of all human organs except those of sex, it may take someone several years to estimate a new kind of form in poetry. It took a lot of people's ears, including mine, a long time to hear the power of the whole unusual context of noises, the fresh form of poetry that John Berryman had been writing since 1938. I know of no experience more intoxicating to the mind than suddenly hearing a new kind of noise in a poet. Even today there is still a special excitement about Laforgue. A fresh rhythm creates its own opportunities. Hearing a rhythm we know already, we are drugged by recollection; we think we know what to expect. There is a given tradition of kinds of poetry, a set of meanings attaching to given rhythms, which an individual poet may alter or modify. But Milton means you to know he is writing a kind of epic. Even in his madness Christopher Smart wants you to understand he is writing a kind of scripture, a kind of psalm.

Consider the verse forms of the metaphysical poets. Is there something specially appropriate to the subject-matter in the noise they make? A soft inevitability, like a fall of thick, heavy snow? An emptiness like an eighteenth-century marble monument that chills you while it inebriates? *O sobria ebrietas, O ebria sobrietas.* Yet George Herbert fills those rhythms with something intimate and familiar. You are more conscious of the brotherhood of the poet than of all the metaphysical distances he describes. In Henry Vaughan there is a marvellous coldness and sweetness. The fall of his verses creates an expectation of death in the last line.

> . . . shew me his life again
> At whose dumbe urn
> Thus all the year I mourn.
>
> ('I walkt the other day')

The rhythm has something in common with Hardy, and they have in common their greatest virtue, a human integrity of language and reasoning, an honesty that minimally fills the outline of their rhythms.

The English language has rejected greater poets, but it cherishes Hardy and Vaughan. I believe there is something of the same quality in German about the late lyric poems of Brecht, a relation of the honesty of the voice to the rhythms of the German language, so that the noise those poems make is something better than we hoped for, a perfectly honest and decent human voice. I think that the secret of the wonderful poems of Kavafis in modern Greek, which are extremely odd from a linguistic point of view, is also in his rhythms, in a compelling honesty that can be heard by anyone who knows the language. We have seen that knowing a language is a difficult idea. It is not necessarily knowing or habitually using most words, though it may include that, and it is certainly not translating into other languages. Knowing is not necessarily conscious or scientific. It must be a kind of selective hearing, a skill of the ear more than the tongue, an understanding which must at some level be intuitive of how language relates to life and reality. Poetry is about reality, but its material is the whole language. The most naive writer may at some time be the best, because he may be the truest. The best poet is certainly the one nearest to the bones of his language, its noises, its points of growth, its particular strength, its proverbial wisdom, its prophetic and sacred texts, the points where it comes closest to reality. If this is true, then the best poet is inevitably a national poet. He is the one who best conveys, whether intentionally or indirectly, the society that made his language. The fact that his subject-matter may be far-reaching is really determined by his marriage to the language itself. The rhythms of poetry expect the whole language in a heightened form, and in his poems he fulfils that expectation. The rhythms of poetry are a provocation to the truth.

Of what we assume to be the three greatest poets, Homer, Dante, and Shakespeare, we know too little about the first and too much about the third for this mechanism to be obvious. They have in common that each of them chooses a vast, remote material, each is supremely Greek, Italian, English, so that we seem to hear the whole force of the languages themselves, and they convey the reality of their own times much more strongly than you would expect from their superficial subject-matter. All three generate the illusion of having created their language. Dante succeeds partly by naivety, by an undeviating system of rambling, interlocking rhymes which he fills now in one way, now in another, sometimes it appears quite by hazard, sometimes for long passages with the subtlest accuracy and the finest eloquence. The result is a variety of tones in the language almost equivalent to the variety of dramatic tones that Shakespeare worked out in the theatre. The noise of Dante is not a level hum. He can transform himself within one line, or slowly, line by line and canto by canto. It seems clear for example that after the *Inferno* he took several cantos to acclimatize himself to the milder shades of purgatory. In some ways Dante is an appalling poet to read, but you forgive him everything for the sudden sharpness of certain lines, and for the personal despair which is the root of his poetry. His poetry is surely not the great and satisfying intellectual construction we all of us failed to understand at school. He is more like a medieval Italian architect, he takes his material wherever he finds it. Think of the extraordinary classical fragments with which he embellishes the twelfth canto of the *Purgatorio*. What is a Greek giant doing in purgatory when his brother is in a low circle of hell? In that canto classical and romanesque are the same to him. Or what about the pink and white cheeks of dawn turning yellow as she gets older? The vitality of his poetry is the way he knows the language and what it can do. It is the Italian language, not a conception of hell or purgatory or heaven, that fulfils every expectation of rhythm, on a great and a small scale. That is how it comes about that in visiting those three remote provinces what he chiefly revealed was contemporary Italy. Before he was halfway through the *Divine Comedy*, and maybe much earlier, I believe he knew that is what he was doing.

The supposed breakdown or intermingling of forms and styles that has followed the modern movement in Europe and America is nothing but an attempt to recapture such vast areas of language and reality as these. John Berryman and Robert Lowell, Ezra Pound and W. H. Auden have been among the great recent examples in our language. I still believe Eliot may be the most important, if only because I find myself continually quarrelling with his ghost. His own line applies to him: 'Even what they had no speech for, when living, they can tell us, being dead.' In all these writers the noise of the verses is paramount, it is what you hear, but the satisfaction of fulfilled rhythms creates a sense that this is how the language works, this is how reality is. The only comfort in poetry is the sense that the world is real and that reality can be expressed. But the most obvious characteristic of modern poetry is great technical freedom. The noises and rhythms are unpredictable outside a given poem. The images are often disordered or unexpected, but today nothing is surprising because everything is permitted. The point was sharply made by John Wain in an important lecture on 'Alternative Poetry' which would be tempting to discuss at great length. Yet even when poetry comes close to a highly mannered sort of prose, it can be heard as poetry. The noise of it puts what it says under a certain tension, however obscure; there are hints of a likeness to other poems, the rhythm liberates a power. The most extravagant surrealism has something in common with the ancient poetry of ballads: one of the Sephardic ballads for example is about a man with three knife-wounds in his neck; through one goes in the sun, through one goes in the moon, and through the smallest out and in goes a worm. In Lorca surrealism and popular poetry come together, and that is why even a foreign ear can pick up the powerful tones of his poetry. The technical freedom he allowed himself was not striking, but his deeper technical originality was astonishing. The originality of poets has often consisted of quite small or at least quite simple changes. It may be in the particularity of a rhythm, the taste for a kind of word.

A poet today, as John Wain has said in his lecture, chooses his limits, he chooses his own voice. He chooses the noise he makes with the language he speaks. Anything is permitted but something has to be chosen, and the growth of a poet is a series of these choices. What has been achieved in this century in English and in French is freedom from a certain kind of very regular stress-rhythm. The result is the opportunity of a new tone, and to pay more attention to other sound-values, and to the way the common language runs. We have been liberated from the necessity to rhyme and from the mossy tones of Tennyson and Arnold, but not from that attention to the noises of the language or that unlearnt knowledge of the language in its bones and roots and behaviour which have always been essential to poetry. We are not only allowed a wide range of choices, we are condemned to it. A modern poet is characterized by the mere individuality of his voice as a stubbornly personal, private figure. There is no common style and little common tradition. We are in a class-divided society and we must do our work in it. In this dumb-show of poetry, we must liberate the energies of the language of our society.

The noise that such a poetry will make is an ordinary human noise. The rhythms that define poetry are not necessarily insistent. In many remarkable poems they underlie what is humanly expressive almost inaudibly.

> Frères humains qui après nous vivez,
> N'ayez les cuers contre nous endurcis. . . .
>
> (Villon: 'Ballade des pendus')

[Human brothers who live after us,/do not have hearts hardened against us . . .]

In this poem each of the three stanzas is ten lines long and consists of a single sentence. The rhyme scheme is elaborate and carries right through the thirty-five lines of the poem in only four rhymes, two of which half-rhyme together. Yet all this is so uninsistent that it has to be specially looked for to be noticed. The noise the poem makes has a slow, serious, descending, resinous tone. It has the human inevitability that such a form can perfectly suggest, but the rhymes and the line-endings are not hammer-strokes and the repeated refrain has an almost anonymous authority:

> Mais priez Dieu que tous nous vueille absouldre.

> [But pray God to forgive us all.]

So far as I know the combination of this form of the ballad with this terrifying subject-matter in such a serious poem is absolutely original to Villon. One can see in his own seven years of recorded development how this poem became possible. His originality is that of a very great poet.

We are not going to find another Villon very easily, or another Brecht, or another Eliot. Poetry has no history, but it alters just as human societies do. Yet languages are slow to alter. Nations change utterly or disappear, but languages are as indestructible as grass. The English language is now probably the most widely spoken on earth. American English and insular English are one language but very different; at least at present they produce different kinds of poet. This is not necessarily a question of merit; one might prefer the abundant energies of American English and American poetry or the laconic power of the insular language and its insular poetry, but a poet has to write more or less in his native tongue; it is in that language he will have to prove every borrowed phrase and every foreign style. The wide diffusion of English in these years makes a deep knowledge of English problematic. A language is everything that could be said in that language. It is a common creation of everyone who has spoken it. It may be that now the time has come for English to sink into provincial traditions. It is prudent to fear metropolitan fashions and international styles in poetry. But in a sense there is only one English language: it can no longer be defined as King's English. We have to speak our language as it should be spoken, yet only the long-suffering language itself in the course of time can define that 'should'. American and insular poetry in English reflect very different societies, and it may be the true choice is social and political.

Perhaps the problem is really moral, and failures of language are moral failures. Poetry can be discerned by what it sounds like, and the quality of a passion, even in the procedures of reason, is apparent in any language. There was always something phoney about fascist art. The way we write poems is as much a part of our behaviour as the way we talk: only that a poem has no protection of privacy. It is already a pretension to speak in a poem; that must be justified by the weight or the force or the piquancy of what is said. The rules of how to speak are those that govern all decent behaviour, even above the privileges of passion, even above the privileges of reason. There are things it is not decent to say, ways it is not decent to talk. These rules have to do with the coherence of society, they alter with the times. The problem of poetry today in the English language is how to behave decently in these times.

It must by now be clear enough there is no best kind of poetry. The two most favoured candidates for the best kind can both be ruled out for different reasons. Epic poetry is the obvious candidate, but that can be ruled out, unless the word 'epic' is used in so wide a sense as to become meaningless, because of the limitation of epic values and epic subject-matter. The state of society in which epic poetry had its greatest flexibility and versatility, in which it altered from performance to performance, lies at the back of most literary, perhaps even of most human development; but we can no longer reach it, and the later developments of western poetry have not been worthless. The other and the more popular candidate for the best kind of poem is whatever is sublime, whatever is uplifting, whatever seems to offer an intuition of the dignity of the universe. But that kind of poetry is suspect on philosophical grounds, and it leaves out too much of human life. Its typical fault is to feed the self-importance of an élite. It encourages readers and writers to pride themselves on high-mindedness, a dangerous procedure.

Yvor Winters tried in his way to break loose, and some of the things he said about poetry are memorable and sympathetic. There is always something attractive as well as something wrong-headed about neo-classicism in any art, because it involves a gratuitous principle of organization.

> A poem is what stands
> When imperceptive hands,
> Feeling, have gone astray.
> It is what one should say.
>
> ('On Teaching the Young')

This verse is not quite redeemed by the last line. Winters fails as a theorist by setting intellect against feeling in a manner contrary to what we know of our psychology, and flat contrary both to the mass of existing poetry and to common experience of the procedures of speech. It is not at all true, though it exaggerates a grain of truth, that

> The poet's only bliss
> Is in cold certitude—
> Laurel, archaic, crude.

This position of the poet is too contrived, but it is worth thinking about. Poetry as a peeling-away of phoney echoes, poetry as the paring-down of a piece of wood, poetry as the wilful achievement of getting something absolutely right, so that the words stay in place on the paper: there is something to be learnt here. But what about the world, what about the reality which is the subject-matter of every art? Poetry is not cold, it is not made of iron. The ambiguities in my first quotation are frigid. The echo of Milton's 'Lycidas' which I seem to divine in the second is inappropriate if one is proposing an ideal of cold certitude.

Poetry is a more natural activity, and genius, which is often based on anonymous craftsmanship, is a much more everyday phenomenon than these quotations suggest. We must always go back to the same begin-ning: the social and moral expectations built into poetry are those of every given language, because poetry is only language under a certain tension. Cold certitude is not the object of all language, although the expectation of economy and a certain restraint are inbuilt into most modern languages, at least in sophisticated countries, and perhaps more finely into 'primitive' languages. There is a certain austerity of concentration about Zulu praise-poems. There is a certain economic strength even in the dazzling rhetoric of *Igor's Raid*. When Kavafis was asked why he had neglected variety of metrical schemes in his poetry he replied: 'My dear, why should I take this pointless trouble? Perhaps you think poetry is something technical, and that it doesn't live the natural life of every art? You'll say: "What about the verse?" But doesn't that exist in our conversation? What is most of our talk but verse, and iambic verse?'

Of course the relations of poems with the given rhythms of the language can be varied in many ways, and even the ground-rhythms of the language itself will alter over centuries, as for example the noise made by the Greek language altered enormously under the Roman empire. The good kinds of poetry at a given time, for example in these modern times, will have a close relation to the living language. That means a noise that can be picked up only by the ear, and a moral resonance that will have to be tested intuitively as well as analysed logically. From the point of view of some kinds of drawing, the emotional content of music is an impurity, and from the point of view of music the moral explicitness of poetry is an impurity. But in using words at all we are doomed to be articulate, and one art should not aspire to the state of another. Poetry should not drift off into a musical dream. Its roots in reality are the roots of language. A poem is a semantic system, modified by a special and self-contained process of noises: but these noises are the essential materials of a given language, and they have their suggestive and semantic force independently of any individual.

Although there is no best kind of poetry, and although it follows that nobody can legislate about the best kind to be written now, poets do in fact want to deepen and broaden their own art. There is a contradiction here which every poet works out in his own way. A poet after all will inevitably recognize his own limitations, and even if he is breaking himself up in words, he cannot be continually breaking his whole style to pieces. He may do so three or four times in a lifetime, but it is almost usually true that a great poet in his maturest work is using opportunities he himself as a young man has created. Philip

Larkin for example has contrived an astonishing range within his own severe limits.

> What calls me is that lifted, rough-tongued bell
> (Art, if you like) whose individual sound
> Insists I too am individual.

> ('Reasons for Attendance')

Something similar can be said about the late lyric poetry of Bertolt Brecht. One can see in Brecht's late poems how he depends on his full and flamboyant dramatic work, and at the same time on the fineness of such famous early poems as 'Concerning Poor B.B.', which was written as early as 1927, though its prophetic truthfulness makes it look much later. There is a late poem called 'Sounds' ('Laute'), for example.

> Später, im Herbst,
> Hausen in den Silberpappeln grosse Schwärme von Krähen
> Aber den ganzen Sommer durch höre ich
> Da die Gegend vogellos ist
> Nur Laute von Menschen rührend.
> Ich bin's zufrieden.

[Later, in autumn,/big flocks of crows lodge in the silver poplars/but all summer through I hear/when the ground is birdless/only the sounds of people stirring./That suits me.]

Such a poem uses up its form utterly; it uses both the marrow and the edges of the form. Its rhythm is so nearly natural that it hardly disturbs the tranquillity of the reader's ears, and yet the final casual-looking line so perfectly fulfils the rhythm that only at that moment can one hear what the form is, and one does, at that moment, completely hear it. The poem creates a silence around itself; it is also a completely realistic poem. It certainly has the individual sound Larkin was talking about, it is certainly also 'what one should say'; yet no one could call it 'Laurel, archaic, crude'.

What poetry feeds on is the resources of language; they include of course the resources of existing poetry. Modern poets in every age have cannibalized old poems. A friend has recently pointed out to me that Byron cannibalized Pope in just the way that Pope cannibalized Chaucer. All that can be said about a best in the movement of poetry, or of the trailing processions of poets, is that the best styles of poetry will express most of reality. At the present time it is evident that many resources of the past are unavailable. But forms are always mixed forms, and what remains unusable in its pure form, Elizabethan tragedy for example, may well take on a new life in a bastard form. The tragedy of Shakespeare was of course already a bastard form, and so was the tragedy of Aeschylus. Reality is more important than purity in this context.

The little poem 'Sounds' is enough to show that the bareness and lack of luggage of humanly honest poetry today do not necessarily entail any formal impoverishment. There has been a feeling about that the great experiments were made by the last generation, by the founding fathers of the modern movement, which was international. It was felt that for better or worse we were in for a period of strict and sober consolidation. But the great opportunities of modern style can be tested only against reality and against real languages. That is true of writers as different as Brecht and Eliot, who did share something perhaps in the twenties, and true of so purely American a writer as William Carlos Williams and so purely Russian a writer as Pasternak. There is a coarse and tenuous sense in which the business of poetry is always the same, even though every element in the formula is constantly shifting; what alters is language, and the human pressures that constantly re-model it. It is far more startling that poetry is so similar than that poems are so diverse; the surprising similarity is not something learnt, but rather re-invented from recurring elements.

In some of William Carlos Williams' poetry the poem becomes strangely moving at a point where permanent or at any rate highly traditional realities focus down onto one sensuous and specific image, and then at the same time these realities confront an impermanent political idea. A cathedral or a stone axe have no divine right to a greater claim on my attention than a tattered poster, either inside or outside a poem. It is the work of literature to bring as many as it can of the fragments of our experience, all marinated in the memory and desire of individuals, into some concrete ramified set of relations. Within the tense context of a poem less can be done than in *War and Peace*, and if this is to be done at all in a poem it must be done intensely and with a certain authority. What is said is not necessarily deeper, but will be intellectually resonant and the noise it makes will be memorable, because the whole context of the poem will be brought to bear on every

line as it appears, and the ear will hear a rhythm that seems inevitable
by fulfilling barely and perfectly the expectations it arouses.

> We forget sometimes that no matter what
> our quarrels we are the same brotherhood:
> the rain falling or the rain withheld,
> —berated by women, barroom smells
> or breath of Persian roses! our wealth
> is words. And when we go down to defeat,
> before the words, it is still within and
> the concern of, first, the brotherhood . . .
> . . . we who salute the word and would
> have it clean, full of sharp movement.

Perhaps in this poem 'Convivio', William Carlos Williams shows
both his strength and an admissible sort of weakness. This is not one of
his greatest poems, and it would be stupid to judge him by it. It is
perhaps too unified, too little ramified, too euphoric. It is something of
a manifesto poem, not unlike the early poems of Pound; but what he
says in it has a relevance to this discussion. If it is precisely words that
intoxicate a writer then he runs the risk that his single phrases and lines
may be better than his whole poems; that is possibly true of Dylan
Thomas. One ought to establish a quality of thinness about some
modern poems, not those of Thomas necessarily, of which the opposite
would not be density exactly, or complication, but something more
like importance, a human weight of experience. In 'Convivio', I prefer
the line about 'the rain falling or the rain withheld' to the two lines that
follow it. Yet there is a smell of real life about those other two lines,
and one phrase alters its neighbours by force of context. Words have an
order like the grain of wood, their energies are slow and latent. Clean-
ness and sharp movement are fine, particularly if their opposite is some-
thing confused or muddy, but language is more organic, and poetry
ought to be closer to the nature of common language, than this parti-
cular poem insinuates. Dylan Thomas, as other poets have done,
invented his own special language for poetry; it was resonant and
impressive, but at certain critical points it failed him.

Italian hermetic poetry, in which the weight of experience is present
but never stated autobiographically, is an attempt of another kind that
Thomas would have understood. But one would be a fool to judge

poets, let alone poems, by theories, and fortunately for the world not much of poetry is really programmatic, it is almost all mixed. A manifesto is either the way a poem is imagined before it is written, or the convictions of an individual poet or the compromise of a group of poets about how their work ought to be read. The poetry of Lorca appears to be thin sometimes in texture, direct in method, and yet always important at the same time. The poetry of William Carlos Williams on the other hand is abundant and Protean. The poetry of Quasimodo in Italian defies contemporary theory. In all these cases the secret is the relation to the rhythms of the given language. Consider the dark sobriety and melancholy of the first thirteen-line sentence of Quasimodo's wartime poem, '19 January 1944', and then what follows it: 'Qualcuno vive./Forse qualcuno vive.' ['Someone is alive./Someone, perhaps, is alive.'] The same rhythms, this time uncomplicated by any reminiscence of 'le parole nate fra le vigne', are to be heard even more clearly in 'Winter Night' ('La notte d'inverno'), another poem from the same sad period. Surely Quasimodo is an important poet.

In many of the poems of the 1939–45 war in Europe, in Éluard and in Aragon just as in Quasimodo, in Pasternak and Akhmatova, and in a poem on the fall of Crete by George Seferis, there is a human weight that has become rare in European languages since the withering away of anonymous ballads. If all that the early modern movement on the Continent accomplished was to make those poems technically possible, it was worthwhile. They are easier in fact to relate to French and Russian poetry early in this century than they are to English poetry since. And of course at the beginning of modern poetry, sprouting out of the ground seeded by Baudelaire, stands the colossal and paradoxical figure of Rimbaud in his adolescence. Robert Lowell has translated a poem Rimbaud wrote in that summer of revolution when he was not quite sixteen, bitterly ironic in its conception as a complete poem but so strong in its execution that even the opening four lines quoted alone will stand for something:

> You, dead in '92 and '93,
> still pale from the great kiss of Liberty—
> when tyrants trampled on humanity,
> you broke them underneath your wooden shoes.
>
> ('To the French of the Second Empire')

To be 'pale from the great kiss of Liberty' might remotely derive from the picture by Delacroix of Liberty guiding the People; it is a forceful and so far as I know an utterly original image. Rimbaud's style came to exist under high pressure. He woke up to sexuality, to revolutionary excitement, and to many other things at once, and before he was eighteen he had written several of the most powerful poems in the French language. As for the fourth line, it is as concrete as the second. The details of those wooden shoes—'calmes, sous vos sabots' is what he wrote—is impressive in two ways. Poetry by its nature battens on significant detail, like a director's camera, and so does socialism. I am speaking of that socialism which Brecht has taught us to understand.

The poetry of the 1939–45 war was not the same as Rimbaud's in any country, and since 1945 there are springs that have run dry. It is not worth having a war or even a violent revolution in order to have the poems it might produce. What Iris Murdoch has said in a context of philosophy is true in particular of war poetry, that most of what consoles us is false. But any poetry that finds something important to say and is not false deserves more attention, compared to other kinds of poetry, than it usually gets. The last few strong and savage poems written by George Seferis under the Greek dictatorship deserve the close study of anyone who takes the art of poetry and its possibilities seriously. It may incidentally be worth saying that the last powerful war poem I know is one called 'Dead Men's Dinner' ('Nekrodeipnos'); it is a memorial for the dead of the Greek civil war by Takis Sinopoulos. But the poems in which Paul Celan dealt with the worst horrors of 1939–45 must have been written at about the same period. Few of the poems about Nazi atrocities, or about any others, have been as terse or so genuine. I can find nothing to put beside Paul Celan except 'Babiy Yar' by Yevtushenko. Auden, for example, in 'The Shield of Achilles' speaks with the more generalized compassion of someone who spent the war elsewhere. So did Brecht of course, but he has an authentic sense of the war.

> Vor mir kommen die Bomber. Tödliche Schwärme
> Melden euch meine Rückkehr. Feuersbrünste
> Gehen dem Sohn voraus.

> (Brecht: 'Die Rückkehr')

There is some merit in directness about genuine experience, whether in love-poetry or in the poetry of war and revolution. But directness is also oblique, also selective, in a poem as it is in the cinema. Written out as prose these lines of Brecht's 'The Return' might look like the prose notes of a writer, like the notes made by Camus. Yet that is already a selective kind of writing; there is nothing loose here. Brecht was a writer to his bones, and he can no more not write well than Cicero, in a chance letter, can avoid the force of rhetoric. 'Before me come the bombers. Deadly swarms announce my homecoming. Conflagrations go before the son.' Brecht is never quite as flat and never quite as dead-pan as he looks. He had read and observed more than most human beings. Writers feed on other writers, on their styles, on their subject-matter, and on the articulate and also the half-conscious sense of what reality is like that they may find in another writer. Kavafis in his old age in Alexandria had a passion, justifiable on many grounds, for the novels of Simenon. What did he learn there or what did he recognize?

It is not open to us to choose to be Shakespeare, or even to elect a deutero-Shakespeare. With the decline of theatrical poetry we have lost an extensive medium of expression of a world we might still conceive to be real. Poetry is not the only literary art, and as other arts are lopped off from it, the poet becomes something of a specialist, trying by force of economic circumstance to concentrate his art on what the cinema and television and the novel and the modern poetic but non-poetical theatre are unable to effect. At the same time he does and must insist on broadening as well as deepening his art, and it is strange and crucial how often these two processes coincide, but that means refusing to admit defeat and reconquering lost territory. Who for example owns the epic narrative now, the poet, the novelist or (surely) the television serialist? But if pure forms are unproductive, if strife between forms is all the more unproductive, then bastard forms are desirable. There was, it is worth repeating, nothing pure about Shakespeare's theatre.

And still one ought not to be chauvinist about poetry, as if a poet ought to go out and win back such a vast tract of territory as the tele-vision play. That only has to be said for its absurdity to be seen. The point of poetry for a working poet is not that it should be called poetry. Nor is there anything more distinguished about poetry than about other skills. It was Brecht, I believe, who demonstrated this. Poetry is not what used to be called a few years ago an 'ego-trip'. What confronts us is that reality has to be expressed, with any or all of the means at our disposal. The rewards of taking part in this enterprise, about which so far I have been delicately silent, are wildly variable and utterly incommensurate one with another. Plainly in a world organized as ours is on an international scale, the pressures are absurd, and some of them are best minimized by the individual. 'That lifted, rough-tongued bell/ (Art, if you like) whose individual sound/Insists I too am individual' is the criterion of every artist. But what we need is mixed forms, and they must have what Lorca called *duende*.

> The *duende* does not appear if it sees no possibility of death, . . . if it is not certain that it can move those branches we all carry, which neither enjoy nor ever will enjoy any solace.
>
> . . . While angel and muse are content with violin or measured rhythm, the *duende* wounds . . .
>
> The magical quality of a poem consists in its being always possessed by the *duende*, so that whoever beholds it is baptized with dark water. Because with *duende* it is easier to love and to understand, and also one is *certain* to be loved and understood; and this struggle for expression and for the communication of expression reaches at times, in poetry, the character of a fight to the death. . . .
>
> We have said that the *duende* likes the edge of things, the wound, and that it is drawn to where forms fuse themselves in a longing greater than their visible expressions. . . .
>
> But, it is worth emphasizing, the *duende* can never repeat itself, as the shapes of the sea do not repeat themselves in the storm. . . .
>
> The muse of Góngora and the angel of Garcilaso have to relinquish the laurel wreath when the *duende* of St John of the Cross appears, when
>
> > El ciervo vulnerado
> > por el otero asoma.
> > [The wounded deer/appears over the hill]
> >
> > (Lorca: 'Theory and Function of the *Duende*')

And yet the small rose-bushes of a provincial art remain mighty sympathetic. The poets over whose heads the whole world could smash, and who would go on as impoverished members of an older academy, to which they had elected themselves because it was dead, are courageous, decent, and even admirable figures. *Nec vexat cineres horti cultura quietos.* But poetry is unable to stay the same; in this it is like history, to which it is anchored by its roots in the inevitably altering language. If poetry uses archaisms, as Milton did, that is just one of the devices of poetry: it is a variation of the texture of the language, either superficial or profound, which is only one of the elements in that rhythmic context of human language we call a poem. The test of its propriety is the success or failure of a concrete, individual poem. Wonderful poems were written in Latin, for example, in the eighteenth century in England. Thomas Gray wrote at least one Latin poem as good as anything he wrote in English. The poem I mean has some relation however, unless I am mistaken, to the habitual rhythms of English speech, and I have forgotten who said of it, 'Thus might Horace have expressed what Horace could never have felt.'

We want real poetry. We want it genuine, authentic, and what we call great. But it is very hard to say why we need it. It may be that within the system of the given language which is nine-tenths hidden from us like an iceberg, some such need is inevitable and common. In that case it seems likely that those poets whose mysterious tap-root descends deepest in the language will know how to satisfy a need we ourselves did not know existed. It may be that poetry of recognizable authority creates the need for itself; it might be really a new thing we would have to want when someone had invented it. The need may be a simple psychological function of how we want our languages to be. The ability to discern what is real, and what is unreal poetry, which seems to increase by mere experience, by mere trial and error, shows that the need for what is real is inbuilt. Perhaps we have an inbuilt appetite for reality. But more likely, we have an inbuilt appetite for the noise made by poems. All the rest follows from that.

Oxford, 1975

Appendix

A CONTRARY VIEW

Poetry is feeling, confessing itself to itself in moments of solitude, and embodying itself in symbols, which are the nearest possible representations of the feeling in the exact shape in which it exists in the poet's mind. . . . Eloquence is heard, poetry is *over*heard.

JOHN MILL
quoted by M. H. Abrams
in *The Mirror and the Lamp*

AFTER TRYING A CERTAIN BOOK

I tried to read a beautifully printed and scholarly volume on *The Theory of Poetry*, received by mail this morning from England – but gave it up at last for a bad job. Here are some capricious pencillings that follow'd, as I find them in my notes:

In youth and maturity Poems are charged with sunshine and varied pomp of day; but as the soul more and more takes precedence, (the sensuous still included,) the Dusk becomes the poet's atmosphere. I too have sought, and ever seek, the brilliant sun, and make my songs according. But as I grow old, the half-lights of evening are far more to me.

The play of Imagination, with the sensuous objects of Nature for symbols, and Faith – with Love and Pride as the unseen impetus and moving-power of all, make up the curious chess-game of a poem.

Common teachers or critics are always asking 'What does it mean?' Symphony of fine musician, or sunset, or sea-waves rolling up the beach – what do they mean? Undoubtedly in the most subtle-elusive sense they mean something – as love does, and religion does, and the best poem; – but who shall fathom and define those meanings? (I do not intend this as a warrant for wildness and frantic escapades – but to justify the soul's frequent joy in what cannot be defined to the intellectual part, or to calculation.)

At its best, poetic lore is like what may be heard of conversation in the dusk, from speakers far or hid, of which we get only a few broken murmurs. What is not gather'd is far more – perhaps the main thing.

Grandest poetic passages are only to be taken at free removes, as we sometimes look for stars at night, not by gazing directly toward them, but off one side.

To a poetic student and friend: I only seek to put you in rapport. Your own brain, heart, evolution, must not only understand the matter, but largely supply it.

WALT WHITMAN
from *Specimen Days in America*

Further Reading

I have named only the few books which are or have recently been more easily available than readers might suppose. This list is not a manifesto. If any book is either obvious or too hard to find, I have not listed it. The critical books I have named are the merest adumbration. Asterisked titles are or have been published by Penguin.

Guillaume Apollinaire, *Selected Poems** (trans. Oliver Bernard)
Louis Aragon, *Le crève-coeur*
Basho, *The Narrow Road to the Deep North** (trans. Noboyuki Yuasa)
John Berger, *The Success and Failure of Picasso**
Bertolt Brecht, *Poems 1913-1956* (ed. John Willett and Ralph Manheim)
T. Carmi, *The Penguin Book of Hebrew Verse**
Paul Celan, *Selected Poems** and *Poems* (trans. Michael Hamburger)
Aimé Césaire, *Return to My Native Land** (trans. John Berger and Anna Bostock)
Edward Doughtie, *Lyrics from English Airs (1596-1622)*
Roy Fuller, *Owls and Artificers*
Roy Fuller, *Professors and Gods*
Geoffrey Grigson, *The Private Art*
Paavo Haavikko and Tomas Tranströmer, *Selected Poems** (trans. Anselm Hollo and Robin Fulton)
Michael Hamburger, *East German Poetry*
John Holloway, *The Lion Hunt*
John Holloway, *Widening Horizons in English Verse*
Randall Jarrell, *Critical Essays*
*Ben Jonson,** selected by Thom Gunn
Philip Larkin, *Required Writing*
Peter Levi, *The English Bible*
*Lorca,** ed. J. L. Gili
Christopher Marlowe, *The Complete Poems and Translations**
Dimitri Obolensky, *The Penguin Book of Russian Verse**
Anne Pennington and Peter Levi, *Marko the Prince* (Serbo-Croat heroic poems)
Fernando Pessoa, *Selected Poems** (trans. Jonathan Griffin)
*Pope,** selected by Peter Levi

Ezra Pound, *ABC of Reading*
Pushkin, *Eugene Onegin** (trans. Charles Johnston)
*Rimbaud,** ed. Oliver Bernard
George Seferis, *Collected Poems* (trans. Edmund Keeley and Philip Sherrrad)
C. A. Trypanis, *The Penguin Book of Greek Verse**
César Vallejo, *Poemas Humanos* (trans. Clayton Eshleman)
John Wain, *Professing Poetry*
Yevgeni Yevtushenko, *Selected Poems** (trans. Peter Levi and
    Robin Milner-Gulland)
The magazines *Agenda*, ed. William Cookson and Peter Dale and *PN Review*,
    ed. Michael Schmidt

Acknowledgments

For permission to quote from copyright material, we are grateful to authors, their representatives and publishers as follows. Titles of poems quoted are given in the main text.

John Berryman, *His Toy, His Dream, His Rest*, Faber & Faber Ltd; Farrar Straus & Giroux Inc., New York. Copyright © 1968 by John Berryman.

Bertolt Brecht, *Poems 1913–1956*, Eyre Methuen. Copyright © Suhrkamp Verlag, Frankfurt am Main, 1964.

T. S. Eliot, *Four Quartets*, Faber & Faber Ltd; Harcourt Brace Jovanovich, Inc., New York.

David Gascoyne, *Collected Verse Translations*, Oxford University Press.

Philip Larkin, *The Less Deceived*, The Marvell Press; *High Windows*, Faber & Faber Ltd; Farrar Straus & Giroux, Inc., New York (copyright © 1974 by Philip Larkin).

Lorca, *Selected Poems* (ed. J. L. Gili). Copyright © J. L. Gili, 1960. Reprinted by permission of Penguin Books Ltd.

Robert Lowell, *Poems 1938–49*, Faber & Faber Ltd; *Lord Weary's Castle*, Harcourt Brace Jovanovich, Inc., New York; *Imitations*, Faber & Faber Ltd, Farrar Straus & Giroux, Inc., New York (copyright © 1961 by Robert Lowell).

Ezra Pound, *Collected Shorter Poems*, Faber & Faber Ltd; *Personae*, copyright 1926 by Ezra Pound. Reprinted by permission of New Directions Publishing Corporation.

Theodore Roethke, *The Collected Poems of Theodore Roethke*, Faber & Faber Ltd, Doubleday and Company, Inc., New York. Copyright © 1960 by Beatrice Roethke, administratrix of the estate of Theodore Roethke. Reprinted by permission of Doubleday and Company, Inc.

William Carlos Williams, *Collected Later Poems*. Copyright 1950 by William Carlos Williams. Reprinted by permission of New Directions Publishing Corporation.

Yvor Winters, *Collected Poems*, Routledge & Kegan Paul Ltd and the Swallow Press, Inc., Chicago.

Index

Quotations are indicated by italicized page references

Aeschylus, 69, 91
Akhmatova, Anna, 93
Apollinaire, Guillaume, 26
Aquinas, Thomas, 53
Aragon, Louis, 52, 93
Aristophanes, 46, 66
Aristotle, 43
Arnold, Matthew, 85
Auden, W. H., 39, 53, 64, 68, 69, 76, 84
  'The Shield of Achilles', 94

Basho, 26, 28, 36
Baudelaire, Charles, 93
Benjamin, Walter, 52
Beowulf, 62
Berger, John, 13
Berryman, John, 25, 26, 35, 82, 84
  'The Dream Songs', *28*
Bible, 13, 22, 30, 39, 56, 73
Bowra, C. M.
  Primitive Song, 45
Brecht, Bertolt, 11, 20, 36, 48, 70, 83, 86, 95
  'Die Rückkehr', *46, 94*
  'Gesang des Soldaten der Roten Armee',
    49
  'Laute', *90*, 91
Bunting, Basil
  Briggflatts, 35, 39
Burke, Edmund, 39
Byron, 90
  Don Juan, 31

'Ça ira', 60
Cadou, René Guy, *14*
Campion, Thomas, 23, *24*, 25
Camus, Albert, 95
'Carmagnole', 60
Catullus, 25
Celan, Paul, 52, 94
Cézanne, Paul, 44
Chaucer, Geoffrey, 31, 90
  The Parliament of Fowls, 65
Chesterton, G. K.
  'Lepanto', 70
Cicero, 95
Clough, A. H., 31

Cocteau, Jean, 66
Coleridge, S. T., 63
Corneille, 47
Corso, Gregory, 69

Dante, 37, 53, 56, 60, 63, 65, 83, 84
  Divine Comedy, 22, 63
  Inferno, 84
  Purgatorio, 84
Delacroix, 94
Dickens, Charles, 37
Dickinson, Emily, 43
'Dies Irae', 66
Donne, John, 22
Dryden, John, 11
  All for Love, 65
Durrell, Lawrence, 73

Eisenstein, Sergei, 19
Eliot, T. S., 11, 20, 41, 47, 52, 53, 63, 64, 68,
  70, 75, 84, 86, 91
  Four Quartets, 37, 39, *76*
  The Waste Land, 36, 73
Eluard, Paul, 93
Elytis, Odysseus, 12
Erotokritos, 60–62
Euripides, 69

FitzGerald, F. Scott, 25
  The Last Tycoon, 19
Flaubert, Gustave, 37

Gascoyne, David, *52*
Gatsos, Nikos, *11*, 79
Gay, John
  Trivia, 38
Ginsberg, Allen, 20, 32, 69
Goethe, 75
Gower, John
  Confessio Amantis, 31
Gray, Thomas, 97
Gunn, Thom, 20

Haavikko, Paavo, 35, 36
Hardy, Thomas, 31, 32, 35, 38, 41, 47, 56,
  81–83

'Haymaking Courtship', *36*
Herbert, George, 22, 82
Hill, Geoffrey
    Mercian Hymns, 35
Hölderlin, Friedrich, *52*
Hollo, Anselm, 78
Homer, 15, 44, 56, 75, 83
    Iliad, 14, 17, 27, 60, 66
    Odyssey, 27, 60
Hopkins, G. M., 21, 43, 45, 76
Horace, 28, 31, 41, 63, 97
    Epistles, 66
Huchel, Peter
    'Der Garten des Theophrast', *67*
Hughes, Ted
    Crow, 29

Igor's Raid, 89

Jaccottet, Philippe
    'Le combat inégal', *50*
Jakobson, Roman, 73
Jammes, Francis, 14
John of the Cross, St, 22, 23, 73, 75
Jones, David, 35, 39
    In Parenthesis, 32–34
    The Anathemata, 33
Jonson, Ben, 20, 47
    'Allegorike', *43*
Joyce, James
    Finnegans Wake, 32, 33, 37
    Ulysses, 32, *33*, 34, 37, 41
Juvenal, 70

Kahlau, Heinz, *67*
Kavafis, Constantine, 51, 81, 83, 89, 95
Keats, John, 63
Kipling, Rudyard, 21, 70

Labé, Louise, *25*
Laforgue, Jules, 51, 82
Langland, William, 76
Larkin, Philip, 12, 38, 49, 90
    'Money', *50*
    'Reasons for Attendance', *90, 96*
Lear, Edward, 80
Lemprière's *Classical Dictionary*, 63
Levi, Anthony, 47
Lévi-Strauss, Claude, 44
Logue, Christopher, 14

Lorca, Federico García, 55, 79, 85, 93
    'Theory and Function of the *Duende*',
        11, *96*
Lowell, Robert, 35, 41, 50, 70, 84
    History, 20, 29
    Notebook, 20
    'The Quaker Graveyard in Nantucket'
        40
    'To the French of the Second Empire
        93
Lucretius, 63
Lukács, Georg, 13, 52

Makryiannis, General, 60
Mandelshtam, Osip, 68
Marlowe, Christopher, 70, 75
    Tamburlaine, 65
'Marseillaise', 60
Mayakovsky, Vladimir, 28
Middlemarch, 15
Milton, John, 16, 29, 30, 38, 41, 70, 73, 78,
        82, 97
    'Lycidas', *77*, 88
Mitchell, Adrian, 14
Murdoch, Iris, 94

Oxford Book of Modern Verse, 20
Ovid, 63, 70

Pasternak, Boris, 91, 93
Paine, Thomas, 39
Pessoa, Fernando, 35, 36, 51
Pope, Alexander, 13, 31, 73, 90
    Epistles, 66
    imitations of Horace, 41
Porter, Peter, 35
Pound, Ezra, 20, 52, 53, 70, 84, 92
    The Cantos, 33, *39*
    'Au Salon', *21*
    'Commission', *21*
    'Tenzone', *22*
Propertius, 25, 64
Pushkin, Alexander, 56

Quasimodo, Salvatore, *14*, 93

Racine, Jean, 47
Rimbaud, Arthur, 11, 28, 29, 93, 94
Roethke, Theodore
    'In a Dark Time', *69, 75*

Romance of the Rose, 60
Romanos, 27
Ronsard, *43*
Rubens, 16

Sassoon, Siegfried, 38
Seferis, George, 12, 14, 47, 68, 93, 94
Shakespeare, 26, 28, 29–31, 33, 34, 41, 47,
    55–58, 62, 69, 70, 75, 78, 83, 84, 91, 95
  Hamlet, 37
  Julius Caesar, *65*
  King Lear, *38*, 80
  Pericles, Prince of Tyre, 67
Shaw, Bernard
  Pygmalion, 70
Simenon, Georges, 95
Sinopoulos, Takis
  'Dead Men's Dinner', 94
Smart, Christopher, 51, 62, 82
Solomos, Dionysios, 59, 60
Song of Songs, 22
Sophocles, 69
Spenser, Edmund, 16
Stevens, Wallace, 50
Surrey, Earl of (Henry Howard), 31

Tate, Allen, 69
Tchaikovsky, 58
Tennyson, Alfred Lord, 21, 85
  'Tithonus', *29*
Thomas, Dylan, 76, 92
Thwaite, Anthony
  The New Confessions, 35
Trakl, Georg, 51

Valéry, Paul
  'Le cimetière marin', *67*
Vallejo, César, 11
  Poemas Humanos, *48*
Vanity Fair, 15
Vaughan, Henry, 22, 51, 83
  'I walkt the other day', *82*
Villon, François, 22
  'Ballade des pendus', *86*
Virgil, 58
  Aeneid, *25*
Voltaire, 17

Wain, John, 85
War and Peace, 91
Waugh, Evelyn
  Officers and Gentlemen, 15
Whitman, Walt, 69
Wilde, Oscar
  'Ballad of Reading Gaol', 75
Williams, William Carlos, 28, 93
  'Convivio', *92*
  Paterson, 32
Wilson, Edmund, *33*, 34
Winters, Yvor
  'On Teaching the Young', *88*
Wordsworth, William, 76
  The Prelude, 29
Wyatt, Thomas, 31, 56
  'They fle from me', *64*, 69

Yeats, W. B., 20, 39, 41, 55, 61, *81*
Yevtushenko, Yevgeni, 14, 64
  'Babiy Yar', 94

POETICA

1 The Poems of Meleager
  verse translations by Peter Whigham
  prose translations and introduction by Peter Jay
2 The Noise Made by Poems
  by Peter Levi
3 The Satires of Persius
  translated by W. S. Merwin
  with an introduction by William S. Anderson
4 Flower and Song (Aztec poems)
  translated by Edward Kissam and Michael Schmidt
5 Palladas: Poems
  translated by Tony Harrison
6 The Song of Songs
  translated by Peter Jay and introduced by David Goldstein
7 The Early Italian Poets
  by Dante Gabriel Rossetti
  edited by Sally Purcell
8 Petrarch: Songs and Sonnets from Laura's Lifetime
  translated by Nicholas Kilmer
9 The Golden Apple
  edited by Vasko Popa
  translated by Andrew Harvey and Anne Pennington
10 Victor Hugo: The Distance, The Shadows
  selected poems translated by Harry Guest
11 Old English Riddles
  translated by Michael Alexander
12 An Unofficial Rilke: poems 1912–1926
  translated by Michael Hamburger
13 Goethe: Poems and Epigrams
  translated by Michael Hamburger
14 Martial: Letter to Juvenal
  translated by Peter Whigham
  with an introduction by J. P. Sullivan
15 Goddesses, Ghosts, and Demons
  The Collected Poems of Li He (790–816)
  translated by J. D. Frodsham
16 Nietzsche: Dithyrambs of Dionysus
  translated by R. J. Hollingdale
17 The Poems of Jules Laforgue
  translated and introduced by Peter Dale
18 Gérard de Nerval: The Chimeras
  translated by Peter Jay
  with an essay by Richard Holmes